The Contented Lawyer

How to survive and thrive as a lawyer

ALF MACOLINO

ISBN: 978-1-923601-47-5

Published by Vivid Publishing
A division of Fontaine Publishing Group
P.O. Box 948, Fremantle
Western Australia 6959
www.vividpublishing.com.au

NATIONAL LIBRARY OF AUSTRALIA

A catalogue record for this book is available from the National Library of Australia

Acknowledgements

This book reflects my life and experience as a lawyer for the best part of half a century. I would never have survived that long as a lawyer if it was not for the love and support of my wife Anna. I met her when I was halfway through my law degree and she has been with me through the ups and downs of being a lawyer ever since. I could not have done it without her.

A book like this is also a reflection of my many interactions with my colleagues and mentors in the legal profession. Thank you for the lessons and the guidance over the years.

Thank you to the younger lawyers that I have trained over the years and who often said that I should put my sometimes offbeat views on paper for the benefit of them and their colleagues. In particular, thank you to a couple of recent junior colleagues in Jacquie Rochow and Helena Errey-White who encouraged me to write the book as one of my first retirement projects.

Thank you to Helena and our colleague Michael Spencer for their constructive criticism on the manuscript.

And heartfelt thanks to my long serving secretary Karen Crandon who came out of retirement to format and proofread the manuscript.

Contents

1

Why I wrote this book

Lots of reasons.

From when I started Law School in 1974 until my retirement in 2025, I spent over 50 years training for and then practising as a lawyer. I have experienced the highs and lows of legal practice. It would have been lovely to have had this book to occasionally refer to during that journey.

This is a book which reflects my experience in the law. I do not pretend to know much, but if my experience and my thoughts help you become a contented lawyer then the book will have achieved its aim.

So, what is my background in legal practice? I started off with a practice in human misery: criminal law, family law and personal injury claims. I did solicitors' work and as was common in the 1970s and 1980s, did most of my own court work. I worked out that this was not really for me, so I expanded my existing succession law practice and did commercial work doing everything from mergers and acquisitions to contracts and all things in between. I did a lot of work for the property, retirement living and aged care sectors. There was contract drafting and advice but there was a lot of dispute resolution thrown in as well.

I have never practised as a sole practitioner or in one of the large legal firms. I have never practised in the Crown Solicitor's Office. I have never been inhouse counsel. My experience comes from only three firms, a small practice of about six to eight lawyers and then a couple of medium size practices of between 20 and 30 lawyers.

But there are a few things which I have done which have exposed me to the underbelly of what it is to be a lawyer.

I spent about 10 years as a member of the Law Claims Committee of the Law Society of South Australia. This was a committee which reviewed professional negligence claims against lawyers. It taught me a lot about risk management and gave meaning to the phrase: *There but for the grace of God go I.* It also showed me the significant emotional impact on lawyers from clients who needed someone to blame. Sometimes the clients were right! It also showed me the narcissistic side of some lawyers who believed that they could never make a mistake.

I then spent about 20 years on the Lawyers Support Panel of the Law Society of South Australia. This was a panel that helped lawyers on a confidential basis with professional and ethical issues and particularly when faced with a complaint lodged with the Legal Profession Conduct Commissioner. It was an insight into how tough legal practice is and the mental anguish which goes with disgruntled clients.

I have trained, managed and mentored dozens of solicitors in my firms. I was trained, managed and mentored in my early years in practice.

I have been sued for professional negligence - which thankfully settled. I have had complaints made against me - thankfully, none were upheld.

There will be parts of this book which are meaningless for a lawyer working for one of the global firms with thousands of lawyers on the books. There will be philosophies espoused in this book which will be hard to implement if you are in a firm where you are told, “It’s our way or the highway”. But there is much within the following pages which might strike a chord with you and be universally applicable.

It is not a long book. Being a contented lawyer means following some common sense and simple philosophies. You will not find any footnotes or references to deep research or academic papers. What I am putting to paper is my lived experience.

I am not someone who worked everything out early in my career and never made a mistake. I made plenty of them, learnt from them and tried to follow a different path based on what I had learned from making mistakes. That path is reflected in this book.

You will find lots of anecdotes and quite a few sayings reflecting my philosophy on legal practice. Some of the sayings I made up myself but most of them were told to me on my journey through legal practice. The anecdotes are true. Hopefully, I have disguised the identity of participants in the anecdotes. Please forgive me if I haven't!

This book is written by an Australian primarily for consumption by Australian lawyers. I have used a few colloquialisms which should be familiar to Australians. But much of what I have written in this book can apply to any lawyer anywhere in the world. To assist in understanding the colloquialisms, there is an appendix with the standard English explanation.

Being a contented lawyer is a two-way street where the responsibility lies with you as a lawyer and with the legal profession. The attitude of the profession and the way it goes about its business has as much impact on your contentment as your attitude to legal practice and to life.

There is a fair bit of legal practice management scattered through the pages. Following good legal practice management underpins being a contented lawyer.

You might be tempted to read it in one go in front of the fire on a wintry Saturday afternoon. Or when you are waiting at the airport instead of scrolling on your phone. After you have read it, I hope that you might refer to it in the future as you navigate legal practice.

I expect you to disagree with some but hopefully not all of what I am about to say. You are a lawyer after all, so I would be astonished if you agreed with everything!

Thank you for buying the book. I hope that it will be a rewarding experience for you.

2

Why did you become a lawyer?

I bet that within a couple of seconds of you reading that question, you came up with a oneline answer such as I want to help people, or I am passionate about human rights. Fair enough. We are conditioned to not think too deeply about a fundamental question.

While you are thinking about it more deeply, let me tell you about my own story and it might give you some guidance on answering the question in a bit of depth. Whether you like it or not, the answer to that question will help you become a contented lawyer. In psychobabble, are you congruent with your values? In plain speaking, does your life as a lawyer reflect the fundamental reasons why you became one in the first place?

My parents were Italians from the south of Italy who migrated to Australia in the early 1950s. We lived in Blair Athol, a suburb filled with working class people, many of whom were European migrants. But the migrants were outnumbered by the Australians, many of whom delighted in exhibiting racism towards the new Australians and their children - me included.

It was a happy childhood, but even then, it was clear to me that without education, you were destined to do backbreaking work in a factory, the market gardens or in many other physically demanding occupations. I saw how families struggled to make ends meet financially.

As an Italian family, we always ate well because Mum was an excellent gardener, and we lived off the backyard produce. Even then, in the mid1960s my parents faced a financial disaster not of their own making. Dad started a second fulltime job, so he worked 80 hours a week for two or three years. I saw firsthand what can happen when you have something like a serious accident and your life is financially turned upside down.

On my 10th birthday, Mum told me that we didn't have enough money to buy a birthday present. I still remember cracking the shits, and eventually she bought me a block of chocolate.

I decided that poverty was not for me and that I was going to get a job that paid good money.

Even then, I don't think that the idea of becoming a lawyer had popped into my head. I was intelligent although I was by no means the sharpest tool in the shed. My education was always in the public school system and on my first day in high school we sat an exam and depending on the results you ended up in the A stream,

B stream and so on. I ended up in the A stream and for that stream this included studying Latin and French.

Latin consisted of learning such useful phrases as: *The poets fought the farmers from over the hill with bows and arrows.* Latin has a completely different sequence of nouns and verbs to English. I could not for the life of me work out why it was necessary for us to be taught such an arcane language in the 20th century. It must have been my Latin and French teacher who informed me that Latin was a prerequisite if you wanted to become a lawyer.

I thought - now there's a job that pays a bit of money that I might be able to do as I was good at English and History. I did my best to learn Latin and although I passed it quite well, I decided that if that was what you needed to become a lawyer, there must be other jobs that I could get without learning such an arcane language.

And so, I thought that was the end of it as far as becoming a lawyer was concerned.

The late 1960s and early 1970s were a turbulent time in Australian society. The old and accepted way of doing things was under great social pressure. Banks would not lend money to single women. I was told a few years ago that the Deputy Principal of our high school who was a middle aged single woman had to save all the purchase price for her first house! If you were a single female public servant, you had to leave work when you got married. Australia was involved in the Vietnam war and when you turned 20 years of age and your number came up on the ballot, you were conscripted to go into the Army and fight in Vietnam. Indigenous Australians had only just been recognised as Australians in the Constitution and attitudes towards them were truly appalling.

I could go on, but you get the drift. One of my teachers in 1970 was heavily involved in the Moratorium movement which opposed the Vietnam war and conscription. He was no doubt a card carrying member of the Australian Labor Party. He would often talk about social injustice and the immorality of war. Strangely, it didn't affect our grades as we were a bit more switched on in his classes than normal!

It certainly sparked in me a desire to help people who needed someone to navigate society and the systems which had been put into place by governments to achieve a certain aim. The idea of becoming a lawyer started to gel again. But Latin was still a prerequisite!

However, as luck would have it, by the time I got to matriculation, Latin was no longer a prerequisite to study law. You beauty! However, for reasons which I can no longer fathom, I was doing Mathematics 1 and Mathematics 2 and I was terrible at Maths. I think I would have got the same results in my matriculation Mathematics exams if I had just written my name on the front of the exam paper and walked out of the exam room. The exam marker would have appreciated that.

Although I matriculated on getting excellent grades for the other three subjects there was no way I was going to get into law and so I ended up getting into a Bachelor of Arts degree at Flinders University and set my sights on becoming a teacher.

When I got into university, I was only 16 years old which was a product of going straight from reception to year two, because my primary school teacher thought that I was smart! I might have been smart but not smart enough to miss an entire year of education.

Nevertheless, it eventually proved a bit of a godsend.

1973 was my first year at university doing the Arts degree. Gough Whitlam had been elected in December 1972 as the Prime Minister, and the Australian Labor Party was in office for the first time in 23 years. It was like a massive scab had been pulled off Australian society. University in 1973 was a hotbed of leftwing politics, sexual freedom and underage drinking.

At some stage during that year, I found out that the Law School kept a few places for people who wanted to transfer from other courses and who had proven that they could cope with university life by getting decent grades. That was all I needed to again rekindle the desire to become a lawyer. I studied hard: even reading The Communist Manifesto for the Politics course.

My grades were good enough to get me into the Law School at the University of Adelaide. 1973 was not a wasted year as I got wine, women and song out of my system and hit the ground running in 1974.

Even better, Whitlam had made university education free from 1974. The law degree was an expensive degree, and I am forever grateful for that free university education. I would like to think that over the years I have repaid the generosity of the Australian taxpayer with my volunteer work.

So, for me the reasons that I became a lawyer were to have a job where I had financial security and to advocate for people who could not do that themselves: particularly those from migrant backgrounds for whom Australian culture and systems were particularly confusing.

I know that that doesn't sound particularly altruistic - but it's the truth. I have given you a longwinded story about that because childhood influences and experiences underpin your attitudes in life. I think as you read this book, you will see that some of my philosophies reflect that upbringing.

Now, having heard my story: why did you want to become a lawyer?

3

The first five years are the hardest

If you have been in legal practice for at least six months you will understand the truth of the saying: *Law School teaches you to think like a lawyer, but it does not make you a lawyer.*

However, I suspect that if you have just graduated from Law School, you think that you have been taught how to be a lawyer and understand the law. Fundamental to being a contented lawyer is accepting that Law School only taught you how to think like a lawyer-or more accurately think like an academic lawyer. You have a monumental amount to learn to become a lawyer. It is also fundamental for the profession to understand that and not expect miracles from graduate lawyers.

Why do I say that the first five years are the hardest? Because unless you have been slotted into a firm which uses you as a battery hen to churn out the same type of document or process, it takes about five years before you see similar sorts of matters turn up again on your desk. You can then draw on your experience to sort out that matter. Otherwise, every new matter causes stress because you must work out what to do and sometimes you do not know what to do and neither does the lawyer in the firm who gave you the job.

Young lawyers should also reflect on the fact that academics who teach you at Law School have significant flexibility in what and how they teach a particular subject. This can have an impact on your understanding of a particular area of law and how quickly you can become adept in that area.

In my last year at University, my Mum and Dad wanted to make new wills and because of their limited English language skills, they wanted me to come to the interview with the lawyer. I attended the interview and when the lawyer was asking about the assets of Mum and Dad, he turned to me and asked if they held them as joint tenants or tenants-in-common. Despite having completed the Property Law subject with a good grade, I had no idea what he was talking about. Luckily, I knew that Dad in accordance with Italian tradition owned everything in his own name and I was able to give that answer. Phew!

When I got home, I immediately looked up my book on property law and quickly understood one of the most important distinctions in property law. Why the hell wasn't I taught this at Law School? Good question.

The answer was that the academic who taught that subject spent an entire term on tracing the cases dealing with whether the Torrens Title system was one of deferred indefeasibility or immediate indefeasibility. I am sure that was of great academic interest, but it could have been dealt with in one lecture on the deciding case and law.

Although that rattled me a bit, I still had the belief that Law School had taught me how to be lawyer.

When I graduated, the main way of doing the year of legal practical training before admission as a lawyer was through articles of clerkship. You signed an indenture promising to serve your principal and got paid 60% of the salary of the most junior clerk in the office.

I started my articles just as there was a massive crash in the construction sector. One of the partners of the firm called me into his office and said that he had a job for me. He asked if I knew anything about a worker's lien. Yes, I did. I proudly puffed my chest out and said that this was where a worker who had done work to manufacture something could hold on to the manufactured article until the worker got paid.

In a deadpan voice, the partner said: "*Well that's all very nice Alf but have you ever heard of the Workmen's Liens Act 1893?*". I professed that I had never heard of that Act. He then calmly handed me the legislation, a bunch of precedents and a chapter from a book on worker's liens. He then said the clients were coming in tomorrow afternoon and I needed to get the documents ready by then.

What followed was a frantic afternoon reading one of the most convoluted pieces of legislation that I have ever read with the looming deadline of the client coming in the next day. Let alone that the client had not been paid and was clearly stressed because that would have a knockon effect for his suppliers and cause cash flow difficulties for the client. I was only a little less stressed than the client.

Welcome to legal practice. This scenario has been repeated hundreds of times in my legal career.

So, what is the point of this anecdote? It's an illustration of what legal practice is all about and rather than getting stressed about not knowing what to do, you need to embrace the challenge of using your intellect to work through the problem. Contentment comes from having arrived at its solution using your intellect or going to seek help from a more senior lawyer: but only if you have tried to first work it out yourself. Nothing irks senior lawyers more than junior lawyers coming in asking for help when they clearly haven't thought about the problem and its solution.

How the profession treats junior lawyers and how junior lawyers engage with mentoring and training in the first five years has an enormous impact on whether lawyers enjoy being a lawyer and staying in the profession.

During my articles, one of the other partners in the firm asked me to write a letter of advice to the client. I did so, and I was chuffed at the result.

I went into the office of the partner and sat down and handed him the letter which was about one page long. He got out his trusty red pen and without looking up once, proceeded to amend the letter, reading out to me the amendments as he was going along. There were so many amendments that after he had finished writing in the margins, he turned the page over and kept writing and writing. The colour was draining from my face and all the while I was thinking: "*I am never going to get this caper.*"

At the end of it, he looked up from the paper and over at the ashen faced young person slumped in the chair and said: "*If I did not think you were fucking worth it, I would not waste my fucking time.*"

The colour returned to my face, and I took the amended advice away and reflected on the amendments and why they had been made.

The importance of the partner's response cannot be underestimated. He could have destroyed my confidence in an instant. He could have read the letter and thrown it back across the desk and told me to go and do a better job without me knowing what was wrong with the letter. He could have berated me for having got through Law School and putting up that type of rubbish in front of him. But he did not.

Instead, in his usual pithy way, he told me that I had the skills, but they just needed refinement.

Regrettably, I have seen but mostly heard about young lawyers in that situation being abused and humiliated. It may make the senior lawyer feel good, but what it does is potentially destroy a career. Even if it does not destroy a career, it may mean that a potentially good junior lawyer decides to go to a different firm.

This is a good example of where the profession needs to train and mentor junior lawyers with empathy. That will lead to many more contented lawyers. It doesn't mean that you cannot be a hard taskmaster and expect decent quality work. It just means that you achieve that by being clear, fair and firm with the junior lawyers.

When training junior lawyers, I always say to them: "*I will tolerate any mistake - once.*" It really sets the bar. It means that junior lawyers know that they can make a mistake, but they need to learn from the mistake and not repeat it.

Conversely, if you are a junior lawyer and you are making the same mistake repeatedly, you need to reflect on why that is the case. It may be that this is the clarion call that legal practice is not for you or that the area of law that you practice in is not one that resonates with you.

You need to work this out as quickly as you can. You may think that senior lawyers in the firm will work out that you are making mistakes repeatedly and show you the door. Some firms do that, but many firms will simply let you wither on the vine by not giving you work or giving you less challenging work in the hope that you will move on. It eliminates the risk of unfair dismissal claims, internal gossip and so on. Better to be stabbed upfront than die the death of a thousand cuts.

If you are going to practice law, then at the end of five years you should assess whether this is for you. By that stage, you have had enough experiences within the law to work out if you can enjoy legal practice and are content to spend the next 40 or so years doing that. If you conclude that it is not for you, make the move at this stage to something else using your legal skills or doing something completely different.

Do not keep going because you think it will get better. Suddenly, you will find yourself in a relationship, with children and certainly with a hefty mortgage. It gets difficult to change course when you are carrying all that '*baggage*'.

I cannot stress enough how important it is for the profession to encourage junior lawyers. A pat on the back for a job well done costs you only a few moments of your time but has an immeasurable impact on the junior lawyer.

After a couple of years of legal practice, I got a job to draft a contract which did not have a specific precedent to follow and involved quite a lot of original thought and drafting. I was certainly not experienced or confident enough to send the contract to the client without one of the commercial partners in the firm settling the document. I gave the contract to the partner who had given me the pithy advice after settling my letter.

It was a long contract, and he took it away and read it and came back into my office with the contract in hand.

I was delighted when he entered the room, and with a broad smile, threw the document back across the desk with the comment: "*That contract is as tight as a fish's arse.*"

Nearly 50 years later, I still remember the comment and how great it made me feel. Leaving the mental imagery aside, it was the standard by which I judged all documents which I drafted and those which I settled.

4

Oh, the stress of it all

It is trite to say that legal practice is stressful.

So many other jobs and professions are too, but the professions of medicine and the law top the list and that is why when people talk about professions they often talk about '*doctors and lawyers*'. You don't hear them talking about dentists and physiotherapists, do you?

I think the reason for this is that more than the other professions, doctors and lawyers are often confronted with not only difficult problems but shifting risks which require prompt thought, judgement and execution. For a doctor it could be a matter of life and death. With lawyers it could be a matter of personal liberty or significant financial consequences.

Whatever the reason, you do not have to be in legal practice for too long to realise that the day-to-day stress is real.

You will never be a contented lawyer unless you accept that stress is part and parcel of the profession and that you need to develop resilient coping mechanisms to deal with it.

After about three or four years of practice, the stress was getting to me. One of my senior colleagues at work was perceptive enough to see the signs and asked how I was going. I was honest enough to say that I was struggling to keep up with the demands of the clients, give the correct advice and all the other pressures that came with being a partner in the firm. In those days, admission to a partnership generally only took a couple of years of legal practice!

My colleague gave me the best piece of advice that I have ever received in nearly 50 years of legal practice.

He said: "*Alf, unless you have fucked it up, it is always your client's problem.*"

Read that sentence again and if there is nothing else that you take out of this book, remember the underlying philosophy of that statement as it will hold you in good stead for the rest of your career.

It's so simple really. We are trained to help our clients with whatever problem society has thrown at them. We do not become the client. We do not have to become the client to help them. If we do the best we can for the client, then we have fulfilled our duty to our client, ourselves, the courts and society.

Once I got that statement through my head, the pressure came off and the stress levels dropped.

That doesn't mean that I spent the next 45 odd years just drifting through the profession in a state of Zen. Every day had stressful moments. But I was able to cope with the stressful moment by following a simple philosophy that at the end of the day, it was always the client's problem.

Conversely, if I did fuck something up, I was completely stressed. And I should have been as lawyers are held to a high standard and if I did not occasionally meet that standard, then I should be held to account.

The underlying philosophy of that statement enables you to assess the client's problem and occasionally give advice which the client does not want to hear. It preserves your independence from the problem. If you have taken the client's position as your own, it is more difficult to do that.

We do not always get to act for the client who has done everything correctly. On most occasions, some criticism can be levelled at the conduct of our client in a matter. If you have become the client or come to align with the client's position, you become stressed when that position comes under challenge from the other side.

It enables you, in cricket parlance, to play everything with a straight bat.

Importantly, it lowers your stress level and enables you to cope with the rigours of legal practice.

In the remaining chapters, I will discuss many issues that cause stress in legal practice and suggest some coping mechanisms. But none of them resonate the way that statement does.

5

Why is my life divided into six minute units?

Indeed.

But it was not always so. When I started out, most firms charged on the Supreme Court Scale of Costs. At some stage, someone in the profession must have worked out that it was fair to charge $X for a one page document, $Y for a letter and so on. It was task based, and lawyers were allowed to charge a specific fee for that task. It differentiated between tasks that required the skill of the lawyer and others that even if the lawyer did the task, they could only charge what a clerk could charge.

There was an hourly rate for interviews and telephone calls. Underlying the concept was that a competent lawyer would take a certain amount of time to do a one page letter and the hourly rate was used to work out what a fair fee would be for that one page letter.

The Scale of Costs still exists and unless indemnity costs are awarded, it is used to resolve costs to be paid by the losing party so that the losing party pays fair costs and it makes no difference if the winning party has used the most expensive legal firm in town.

It required lawyers to know what items existed and how to charge based on those items.

It rewarded efficient lawyers. It encouraged lawyers to implement systems, standard letters, precedents and so on to become efficient. If you could streamline your processes and get more done with the amount of time available, you could still charge the same cost for the item and increase your profit. In short, it encouraged productivity.

But lawyers still had a budget to meet and charging on the Scale of Costs was how you achieved that budget.

When lawyers criticise the time costing system (and there are many valid criticisms which I will deal with later in this chapter) what they are really criticising are fee budgets which cause stress and interfere with having a balanced life outside of the law.

So why did time costing and the dreaded six minute unit become so entrenched in the legal profession? I blame the accountants. Initially, it started as a way to measure productivity. For example, if a task such as writing a two page letter took someone two hours but you could only charge for effectively one hour on the item costing system under the Scale of Costs, then that lawyer was unprofitable and 'unproductive.'

At some stage a bright spark worked out that rather than divide one hour by 60 minutes to have one minute units you could divide one hour by 10 to have six minute units and then tell clients that if a job took seven minutes you could charge them two six minute units rather than seven one minute units. It meant that you could charge for more hours than you had worked and this would increase your profit. Pure genius, don't you think? It beggars belief how the profession got away with this deal and managed to get it entrenched not only with clients but also with the current Scale of Costs.

Although the previous paragraph is a cynical view of it, I think the real reason that it became entrenched was that it was an easy management tool for firms to implement. As more firms in the 1980s employed nonlawyers as managers, they wanted a simple way to work out budgets and then monitor performance against those budgets.

Working out the overhead budget is relatively straightforward, particularly for firms which have been going for a while. Unless the firm is in a significant growth phase, the overheads are generally the same as the previous year but increased by inflation and couple of percent for unforeseen circumstances.

Working out the income budget when you use the item costing approach requires a degree of foresight and judgement. It requires you to think about where the work has been coming from, whether that is going to continue, what areas of work are more profitable than others, what the competition is up to, can we increase productivity and so on.

It requires you to work out what you will pay partners for notional salaries and then work out what is a realistic profit for how hard the partners want to work and to get a decent return on the equity they have invested in the firm. If there is no decent return on equity, why would you own a firm?

In theory, if you use time costing you should be doing the same exercise. However, it is much simpler to say that the hourly rate of the lawyers based on experience is $X and each lawyer must charge Y hours per day. We have Z lawyers. So X multiplied by Y multiplied by the number of working days in a year multiplied by Z and as easy as that, you end up with an income figure. After payment of notional partner salaries, is that enough profit and return on equity for the capital partners to be happy and remain with the firm?

And it makes it easy when at the end of the month, the management of the firm can simply go to a lawyer and say your budget was set at $Z and your work in progress for that month was $Z less 10%. Why is that the case? And on it goes …

Of course, the above is an overly simplistic analysis, and the setting of budgets should consider other roles that a lawyer might have to play such as being on the management team, being responsible for business development and so on.

The time costing approach also makes it efficient for management to work out the budget without input from the lawyer who must meet it and impose the budget from above. Both approaches to costing in theory require management to engage with the lawyer who must meet the budget and ask questions such as how much work is available, what are the prospects of getting that work, do you have capacity to do that work, do you have the expertise to do that work and so on.

And there lies the rub of the matter. Once a firm gets to a certain size, the management time that must be invested in setting the income budget for each lawyer becomes unmanageable. Far simpler to take the time costing approach and lawyers can take it or leave it.

What that approach fails to appreciate is that the lawyer (and it can be an employee or a partner) has no control over one of the most fundamental things in life - how hard you must work to earn an income. That loss of control causes stress and great discontent amongst lawyers.

But budgets are necessary so that an appropriate income can be earned by both partners and employees. Doctors must see so many patients per hour. Motor mechanics must service so many cars per day. We are not alone.

My first firm used item costing, and my last two firms used time costing. Entire books have been written about the failings of time costing, and indeed even item costing. The books suggest alternatives available to us.

This book is not the place to do a detailed analysis of the pros and cons of various costing systems. However, I have seen lawyers under pressure to meet budget use all sorts of creative ways to inflate the timesheet. I have seen inefficient lawyers survive because they put it on the timesheet, it gets billed and it gets paid.

I think the general feeling about budgets is summed up by a comment which I made on LinkedIn in response to a post that an international law firm had just set budgets for its lawyers at eight chargeable hours per day.

My comment said:

I have been a lawyer for over 46 years. I have enjoyed being a lawyer and made a decent living. I have enjoyed the company of family and friends over the journey. I have raised two great children and I'm still married to the girl that I met when I was in Law School when I was 19 years old. Try doing all of that if you have to charge out eight hours a day. To do that you have to be sitting in front of the computer screen for at least 12 hours a day. Don't spend an inordinate amount of your life making someone else rich.

It went viral. No one disagreed.

But the elephant in the room is artificial intelligence. At the time of writing, artificial intelligence has only been mainstream for a couple of years, but what it can achieve is mindboggling. It will only get better. There are massive risk management issues for lawyers such as its ability to hallucinate and its ability to breach confidentiality. But they will be resolved or at least mitigated, even if it is simply lawyers remembering that they need to check the work done by artificial intelligence in the same way that they check the work done by a graduate or junior lawyer.

Artificial intelligence enables work that used to take

several hours to be done in minutes. Even allowing for checking by a lawyer, how can the time costing approach remain valid? A lawyer cannot ethically or contractually charge excessive time to a client or doing a job. We cannot use artificial intelligence and get the job done in 15 minutes and then charge for two hours.

The clients won't let us get away with it and neither should they. But more importantly, tech savvy lawyers will use the technology, and in the knowledge of how much time the job will take, they will move to fixed fee type arrangements.

The legal profession is about to get its biggest shakeup in decades.

Much has already been written about what legal practice will be like in five years' time. Those who embrace artificial intelligence as an essential tool of legal practice, learn how to use it properly and embed it within the law firm will survive and prosper. Those who do not will probably survive but with reducing incomes.

Regrettably, some lawyers will become dispensable. Particularly those who are engaged on routine work. But is that any different to when banks of secretaries typing nonstop were replaced by word processors and then by lawyers who could type or use voice dictation to get their work done?

Is it such a bad thing that artificial intelligence may assist the profession in much of the work that is now regarded as drudgery? I think it will mean that young lawyers (and maybe not so young lawyers) will need to develop critical thinking and analytical skills that will put them in demand. More on that later.

Against that backdrop, I think that the time costing approach will go the way of the typing pool.

Law firms will need to work out a way to charge their work when a proportion of it is done by artificial intelligence. I think an outcome of that might be that lawyers have more control over their budgets and how they work. Law firms will have to work out how to set a budget for a lawyer who uses artificial intelligence efficiently and effectively, how that lawyer's clients are going to be charged, and just as importantly how is that lawyer to be remunerated against one who refuses to use artificial intelligence?

These are difficult questions. The answers to them will significantly impact on the contentment of both the legal profession and its members.

6

Walking the tightrope

Life is a balancing act between work, play, family and friends. The balance is never static. It means different things to different people and sometimes you don't get to choose how to balance the competing interests.

The key to being a contented lawyer is to work out relatively early in your career what the balance is going to be. For some of us, the desires to earn a substantial income and have the trappings of wealth are critical. Then there are some of us who value their health and social relationships above wealth. Most of us are somewhere in between.

The balance between work and life is for you to work out and accept. There is no right or wrong. You just need to understand why you have come to that view.

Importantly, you must be comfortable why you have come to that view. If wealth and status are a priority, then you will be content working in firms which prioritise those aspects of life.

Conversely, if you are of that view but you are working in a firm which prioritises life outside of the law, you will struggle to be content. You will always be looking over the fence and wondering why lawyers in other firms always seem to be driving around in expensive cars and going on overseas holidays. You grow to resent those lawyers.

Legal practice is demanding. Even if you are a well organised, intelligent and efficient lawyer, you need to work hard and work hours which in many jobs would be regarded as punishing.

If you want a job where you can turn up at 8:30 AM and then leave at 5 PM on the dot, then legal practice is not for you.

But we are not alone. Professional occupations such as doctors, lawyers, accountants, architects and so on all require dedication and longer hours than nonprofessional occupations. Of course, there are many nonprofessional occupations that have long hours as well. But one of the historical reasons why the professions are respected in society is that they require a significant expenditure of intellectual rigour and time by the members of that profession.

Being a contented lawyer requires acceptance of that proposition.

Fair enough. But does that require lawyers to routinely work 60 or more hours a week or work throughout the night to meet a deadline imposed by a client who is tucked up in bed? I do not think so.

These requirements are not the sole preserve of the large legal firms. I know of smaller firms who adopt the same approach to work and impose these requirements on their employed lawyers and partners.

I have met thousands of lawyers in my career. I have worked with probably 150 lawyers over that time. Almost without exception, any lawyer that I have discussed work-life balance with has said to me that they wanted to spend less time in the office and more time with family and friends and just enjoying themselves.

So, what are the consequences of not having a work-life balance with which you are comfortable?

When I was in my mid40s, I went to a financial planning seminar and received what I think is the best piece of financial advice that I have ever received. The presenter was asked a question by a member of the audience on what the best financial advice was that he could give to a professional person.

The presenter simply said, "*Go home early and make love to your spouse. The worst financial decision you can ever make is to divide your capital in half and have to start again!*"

After the laughter died down, I remember thinking: geez that makes so much sense. I've handed out that advice to quite a few people since.

The consequence of not taking that advice was amply illustrated when I was having a chat to a lawyer about when he was looking to hang up the tools and retire. He looked at me forlornly and said that he was on his third marriage, and he thought he would have to work until physically or mentally he was unable to do so.

There are many reasons why marriages fail, but prioritising work over your spouse is right up there. If you haven't got time for your spouse (who hopefully at one stage made your heart skip a beat and gave you sweaty palms), then almost certainly you have no time available for your children.

Let alone your other social relationships with extended family and with friends.

Friendships need work. Friendships need you (or you and your spouse) to turn up to social functions. If you are always in the office and don't have time for social activities, invitations start to dry up. Sometimes, you become a self-fulfilling prophecy in that if no one bothers to ask you out for dinner, you end up spending more time working in the office.

Another consequence of not getting work-life balance right is that your health suffers. Our bodies were not meant to suffer the rigours of a sedentary lifestyle with long hours in front of a computer screen. With the exhaustion that often comes with legal practice, it often means that you do not get enough exercise. A disastrous recipe. On top of that, if you do not eat well and you drink too much alcohol or take too many drugs, the recipe turns poisonous.

I know that paragraph is exaggerating to make a point, but I have seen too many examples of work-life imbalance in the profession.

After my attendance at the financial planning seminar, I started to take a bit more interest in the topic - financial planning that is not sex with my wife (I was already interested in that topic). I read an article about the best type of investment. The first part of the article was devoted to a person who had done very well out of property investment, and he waxed lyrical about the benefits of this over share investment. The second part of the article had a successful share investor go on about the benefits of this and why it overshadowed property investment.

But it was the third part of the article that struck home. This person said that he had invested in his health by prioritising exercising, annual health checks, meditating, taking regular holidays and not working too hard!

In the long run, who do you think is going to be better off? Sure, there will be a time when the successful property investor or the successful share investor will be ahead financially, but there comes a time when all the money in the world cannot buy you good health. Far better to be in good health and financially okay then to be in poor health and super wealthy. And do not think that the equation only tilts in favour of good health when you are elderly.

In recent times, I have been getting a feed on my Facebook account which shows a young man interviewing people he has met in the street ranging from about mid60s right through to mid90s. One of the questions he often asks them is along the lines of is there one thing that you prioritised during your life that now doesn't seem to be so important to you? Everyone says that they were too focused on making money in their early life and not prioritising their health and wellbeing.

Of course, it is easy to say that when your health is failing and you are financially okay. Or that you know that you haven't got long to go and you have enough money to last until then! It is a far cry from when you are in your 30s and 40s with mortgages, car payments, school fees and lots of living expenses to pay for.

And so, it comes down to this. My experience in life is that if you want to have a balance between work as a lawyer and the rest of your life, your income will need to be adjusted accordingly in a downwards direction. That does not mean that you live on the poverty line. You can still have a decent living. But the brutal reality of the legal profession is that if you want a high income, you need to work long hours.

I made my choice early in my career. I chose to prioritise my family and my health over making a lot of money. Over the years, I got approaches to join larger firms and smaller firms which I knew had a culture of money first - family last. Had I accepted any of those I probably would have increased my income by 30%. I wasn't prepared to do so. I was content with my income and my life. I wasn't prepared to give those up for some extra money and not have the time to enjoy it.

Sure, there have been many times in my career when I have worked late, been in the office early, worked on a weekend and so on. I accept that this is part and parcel of being a successful and contented lawyer.

But one of the nicest things my children said to me when they became adults was that they always remembered me coming home at 6 PM for dinner with them and hearing the crunch of my car's wheels coming up the gravel driveway. I almost never went back in the office after dinner. I was there for them, and even though they never told me this as little children, they appreciated it.

It vindicated my decision to give up the dollars.

A lot of what is in this book is about how you achieve a work-life balance. Once you have decided about how hard you are going to work to achieve a certain level of income, the object is to become efficient with the time that you are at work so that you can earn a decent living.

No one on their deathbed has ever said that they wished that they had spent more time in the office.

7

Ring fencing your life

Achieving a balance between your work as a lawyer and your life outside of the law takes discipline. You must draw up boundaries and with the odd exception respect those boundaries.

Let me explain. Say that you are prepared to start work at 8:30 AM every workday, have half an hour for lunch and finish by 6 PM, and not take any work home or work on weekends. The rest of the time is yours to eat, sleep, exercise and be with your family and friends.

It sounds simple, but legal practice is not so easily compartmentalised. Clients get themselves into problems which require immediate and urgent action. Existing matters blowup. Personal and family crises in your life intervene. Life is never smooth, and you should not expect it to be so.

But if you have the basic discipline of knowing what

hours you are going to devote to legal practice and you accept that occasionally that's not going to work, you can be comfortable with that. When you must go to the school to pick up a sick child and stay home a bit - just do it. Do not stress yourself that you have had to step outside of the boundaries that you have set.

If you focus on becoming efficient during the time that you are at work, then the blowups and disasters that are part and parcel of legal practice do not upset the apple cart. If your practice is under control, you can more easily cope when the disaster turns up.

The ability to ring fence your life has dramatically changed in my time in the law. When I started practice in the late 1970s, legal practice had not changed much for 50 years or probably longer. All files were paper based. Computers and word processing equipment had only just started to infiltrate the profession and cost significant amounts to buy. Lawyers dictated letters and documents, and it was still common to dictate to shorthand typists. Legal secretaries typed the dictation. There were no fax machines. There was no Internet. There were no mobile phones. All phone calls came through the switchboard. Written communication was by letters. You had to physically search public registers. Most legal offices shut between 1 PM and 2 PM for lunch and even turned off the phones! High-tech firms had a telephone answering machine.

When you look back at that time, you can see that ring fencing your work life from your personal life was much easier. If you were not in the office, you were almost impossible to contact and you were able to keep clients at a suitable distance.

The lessons that I learned from those times continue to have validity despite a rapidly changing technological and client landscape.

It was not always beer and skittles in those days. Going on holiday for a couple of weeks meant working like a dog for two weeks before you went and then working like a dog for another two weeks after you came back. As much as possible, you had to make sure that your practice was up to date before you left. You knew that you could not leave files in the hands of others who knew little about the file and who could not contact you for any clarification.

But that habit is a good one and I followed it for the rest of my practising career. It meant that I knew that it was only blowups and disasters that my colleagues had to deal with when I was on annual leave. They did not have to contact me. It meant that when I was on holiday, I could relax and not think about work.

That habit takes discipline. I have seen the goalposts shift dramatically over the years where colleagues go on annual leave and then spend an hour every morning answering emails, taking phone calls from clients and even drafting letters and documents on the laptop they took with them 'just in case'.

This is sheer lunacy. How can you possibly relax and enjoy the holiday in the company of family and friends when every day you are reminded of what is going on back at work? Once you have been reminded of a problem at work, you are mentally wired to think about how to resolve that problem. That is what we are trained to do.

Discipline rubs off. My colleagues knew that when I went on annual leave, my practice was as up to date as possible. I was showing them respect in that I did not want to leave problems for them to deal with amongst their busy practices. With this knowledge, my colleagues were happy to deal with any problems that did arise when I was on annual leave, because they were the exception rather than the rule. It also meant that when I came back from annual leave, the disasters had been dealt with, and it was a matter of catching up with the routine work that had come in when I was on annual leave.

I have focused on annual leave, because in my experience lawyers never take enough annual leave. Of course, it is much more difficult to take annual leave if you are a sole practitioner. If you follow the above discipline and you have a 'best friends' relationship with another sole practitioner or a firm that you refer a lot of work to, you can get them (with the consent of your clients) to deal with the disasters during your annual leave.

Even sole practitioners can take off three weeks over the Christmas New Year break without the world falling apart.

There are a myriad reasons why lawyers don't take enough annual leave. Law firms should take annual leave into account in setting budgets. But even then, lawyers who struggle to meet budget don't take annual leave and try and make up the budget deficit when they really should be getting some vitamin D at the beach. Maybe lawyers think they are indispensable and that if they are not there to solve a problem, clients will leave or go to another lawyer in the firm. And on it goes …

The best anecdote I heard about not taking annual leave was told to me by a partner in a substantial eastern states law firm. His wife had got so sick of him taking phone calls whilst on annual leave that she booked a holiday house in an area where she had confirmed that there was no mobile telephone reception (in the days when Australia did not have consistent coverage in the regional areas). He said that after suffering anxiety for a couple of days that his clients could not contact him, he realised that the world had not caved in, and he had the best holiday in years.

Ring fencing annual leave is one thing, but ring fencing the daily grind of legal practice is quite another.

Our availability to our clients and our colleagues has gradually infiltrated our lives where ring fencing our lives requires more than discipline. We can never go back the late 1970s and neither should we. Technology has greatly improved our lives and the practice of the law.

What I am about to say is in relation to routine legal practice. It doesn't apply on the day of settlement of a multimillion dollar transaction and doesn't apply when you are in middle of a trial. They are the exceptions.

There are the times when you simply must be available as the case requires. But for routine matters …

When you are at work - you work. I do not mean that you cannot take five minutes to have a chat in the office kitchen about the weather or the footy results over the weekend. But it does mean that you focus on the work to be done and get it done. If you get it done, you don't get phone calls or emails from clients chasing you up. If you get a new job in (these days most of them come by email), acknowledge the work within a few hours and let the client know when you are likely to give it detailed consideration. Note that I said 'detailed consideration' - not completion of the work.

Put yourself in the shoes of the client. They have a problem. They have sought your advice. They have decided to spend money (perhaps lots of it) getting that advice. At the very least, let them know that you are onto the job even if you are not going to be able to complete it immediately. In my experience, clients (unless it is a genuine emergency) are content that you are onto to it and are in the tent with them.

But the other side of the coin is that when you go home in the evenings, on the weekend or just having a day off, you do not check your emails. Either get your secretary to do that and if necessary, contact the client (or you in an emergency) or put the out of the office message on your email system. This level of discipline is not easy. I have seen colleagues who are scrolling emails during CPD sessions and partners' meetings. If you cannot discipline yourself at that level, what hope have you got to not check your emails when you are at home or at a restaurant over the weekend.

But I hear you say: even if you can exercise that discipline with emails, that will not stop clients ringing on the mobile or leaving messages on your direct line which comes through to your mobile phone. Of course it doesn't. But we are not in the life and death business. Most phone calls can wait until the following day. If you have received mobile phone calls on Sunday, ring them back first thing on Monday.

If you are in the fortunate position of working for a firm which does not routinely give out mobile phone numbers to its clients, then only give your mobile phone number to clients who will respect your privacy and the fact that occasionally you are entitled to a life outside the law. My experience is that if you say to a client that you are giving them your mobile phone number because they are a valued client, they respect this and only call you after hours when they really need to. In those cases, take the call - but if the call could have waited until office hours, ask the client why they are ringing on the mobile. The subtle message is that don't bother me outside of the office with stuff that could wait until I am in the office.

In Australia, we now have the legal right to refuse to take phone calls and access emails out of the office hours unless it is unreasonable to do so. That sounds wonderful in theory, but there will still be the subtle pressure from those more senior than you to still be available after hours. Lawyers will still worry that they will be passed over for the next promotion because they do not take phone calls or answer emails after hours.

I get that. However, lawyers who are good at their jobs need to understand that they are in a position of considerable power in the employment relationship. If you are a good lawyer, it is a foolhardy law firm that will jeopardise that relationship just because you have ring fenced your private life and do not take emails or phone calls unless absolutely necessary outside of office hours. Law firms know that you cost a lot to replace. You are a valuable commodity if you have the expertise and the skills that other law firms want. You must have confidence in your own ability to stand your ground. You might be surprised at the outcome.

Technology has enabled lawyers to work from anywhere. Long gone are the days when you had to go into the office to get any work done. The technology that is available now enabling lawyers to work from home is brilliant. But for all the advantages that working from home brings, it brings numerous challenges in balancing work life and nonwork life.

Hybrid working from home and from the office is here to stay and law firms that do not embrace the concept will eventually be left behind. But there are a few rules and concepts which need to be put into place for hybrid working to benefit lawyers and the law firm.

The rules of confidentiality still apply whether you work from home, in a café or in the office. The importance that clients place on confidentiality was vividly brought home to me some years ago when at an internal CPD session a couple of clients had a question-and-answer session with the managing partner. The managing partner asked each client what would cause them to change lawyers. Before the managing partner had time to direct which client should answer first, in unison they both said: "*a breach of confidentiality*".

It beggars belief that lawyers will discuss confidential matters on the telephone in a café, type confidential letters in full view of others having a cappuccino and even leave the computer on at home when friends or neighbours come over for a chat.

When you take that into consideration, working in public spaces is not on. If you are going to work from home, then a dedicated area is required. It is one thing to use the dining room table during the Covid 19 pandemic and quite another to use it on ongoing basis.

In the context of ring fencing your life, you need to be able to close the door on your home office and not be constantly reminded of the work spread out across the dining room table. If you do not have a home office, then you need to be able to pack up and tidy up the area that you use for work. At least make it a bit difficult to have a quick look at the emails!

Working from home requires even more discipline than just going to the office every day. The practice of the law often requires concentrated thought. That is very hard to achieve if you do that work in the middle of family life with the washing machine going, dinner on the stove and your children watching TV or playing video games on their devices. You would not allow that to happen in the office, so why allow that to happen at home?

I used to say that '*rent was a small price to pay for sanity*'. Maybe it is counter intuitive, but that saying applies as much now, because there is little point in working from home if home life is chaotic and stressful. Much better to pay the rent and get a bit of sanity in the office environment.

The key word in the phrase 'work-life balance' is 'balance'. The office has advantages which are difficult, too expensive or impossible to replicate at home. Reception areas, administrative support, meeting rooms, significant printing and scanning facilities and so on have been developed for a reason. They are an efficient use of resources. The collegiate nature of working in a law firm where you can discuss issues, learn by osmosis and socially interact should never be underestimated.

Conversely, the removal of commuting to and from work, and the ability to get work done without interruption make working from home attractive.

There is no right or wrong way to approach this issue. You must work out what is the right balance for you. Law firms need to work out what is the right balance for them. When those opposing forces find an acceptable balance, productivity and contentment follows. Dictatorial approaches by both law firms and individual lawyers will end in tears.

8

Don't forget the secretary

For decades, the pinnacle of the secretarial world was being a legal secretary.

And for good reason. As a rule, lawyers could not type but produced prodigious amounts of dictation which had to be accurately transcribed and typed by efficient secretaries. Lawyers' reputations rested on the accuracy of their documents. Before word processors, secretaries had to be incredibly accurate. If they stuffed up typing a will, they could not 'white out' the error and type over it. They had to start again. You could tell when the secretary had done this because they would rip the sheet of paper out of the typewriter with gusto and quietly swear under their breath.

No lawyer wanted to be criticised for having made a 'typo'. On one occasion, I had to apologise to a judge for a 'typographical error' in a pleading. The judge tersely replied, "*Mr Macolino. There are no typographical errors. Only settling errors.*" Indeed.

When I started legal practice, it was common to have one secretary for every two lawyers, and some busy practitioners had one all to themselves. A top-quality legal secretary made life so much easier for a lawyer. Very often, they were very intelligent women (I have only encountered two male secretaries in nearly 50 years of practice) who in today's world would almost certainly have gone to university. And the good ones did more than just type - they dealt with some client queries, drafted simple letters and basically organised a busy lawyer's life in the office.

Life as a legal secretary gradually changed over the decades. The advent of word processing software, computers and lawyers who could type either by hand or by voice dictation dramatically reduced the reliance that lawyers had on legal secretaries. By the time I retired, I was sharing my secretary with six other lawyers.

By now you must be wondering why I am reminiscing about secretaries and the important role that they play in a lawyer's life.

I have heard that there are some law firms that have no secretarial staff and rely on the lawyers to produce the documents and do all the administrative tasks as well.

Not having any secretaries or not having enough secretaries is not in the interests of the wellbeing of a lawyer and limits being an efficient lawyer.

Let me explain. I was not an oldfashioned lawyer

who sat in the office dictating into a dictating machine with a secretary outside the door transcribing and typing like her life depends on it, getting me cups of coffee and filing mountains of paper into files.

I cannot type or at least I cannot type at a sufficient speed to cope with legal practice. About 20 years ago, I began to use voice dictation software. I use the best in the business called Dragon Naturally Speaking which has software specifically designed for use in legal offices. This book has been written using it.

I had run electronic files for about the last 15 years of my time as a lawyer and had as little paper in my office as was realistically possible.

As for my secretary sitting outside my office. Totally unnecessary. They say that necessity is the mother of invention and so it proved to be with two of my secretaries.

About 20 years ago, my then secretary fell in love and married a dairy farmer who lived about 90 kms south of Adelaide. After she married and moved to the dairy farm, she continued to travel to Adelaide every day for work. Within a couple of months, it was obvious to me that this was taking a significant toll on her. I suggested that she work from home two days a week and we could use the recently installed digital dictation system to send dictation and typing back and forth. It worked a treat, and she remained my secretary until the birth of her first child.

Cupid struck again about eight years ago when my secretary (a different one by the way) met and fell in love with an Adelaide man who was about to retire to Batemans Bay on the far south coast of New South Wales. She wanted to go there and live with him but still be my secretary. At her suggestion, I set her up in a home office and because I used voice dictation to do the initial draft and I ran electronic files, we were able to seamlessly work this way for over six years. Clients could not believe it when they realised that my secretary was 2000 kms away.

When the Covid 19 pandemic sent us all to work from home it was literally plug and play for me and my secretary.

As time went on, I did more of my own documents using voice dictation. It was no big deal because I was used to dictating with my voice into a dictating machine and the voice dictation software typed at around about 150 words per minute with 95% accuracy. My secretaries became my proofreaders. But because they were also highly skilled in word processing, they could do things with the documents to make them robust which were way beyond my skill level.

The point of those anecdotes is that lawyers who want to have a contented life should respect the skills of their secretaries and work out a balance which plays to your strengths and to your secretary's strengths. You work as a team. I have lost count of the number of times that my secretary has saved my bacon by picking up errors or reminding me to do something.

Even in today's world, good secretaries have some fundamental strengths which support and enhance a lawyer's life. They are very good at Microsoft Word (which is the standard in the legal profession) and can do things with documents which very few lawyers can achieve. Even lawyers who profess to be proficient in Microsoft Word are not a match for a good legal secretary.

Secretaries are excellent proofreaders. They have all copped the brunt of a lawyer pointing out typographical errors in their typing. They learn very quickly how to proofread their typing!

Secretaries are usually well organised. This is one skill that has got better over the years as you can be a bit disorganised when you only have one or two lawyers to work for but when you have six or more, it is chaos if you are not organised.

Intelligent secretaries like to have a challenge and thrive on being given a delegated task that is unproductive for a lawyer to do.

Secretaries can bring all those skills to assist the lawyer. Why not use them? Why not make your life easier?

Lawyers should confine themselves to tasks that are best done or need to be done by a lawyer. If one of those tasks is producing something in writing, why would you bother typing at a pedestrian speed when you can dictate using voice dictation at between two to three times the speed that you can type. *Typing is so 1890s.*

So being a contented lawyer means finding that balance between your skills and those of a secretary. I find it difficult to believe that a highly trained lawyer at the rates that we charge should be doing work that can be done by a secretary at a significantly lower cost. And just as importantly, the skills of a good secretary enhance your skills as a lawyer.

9

Brand Equity

You have not stumbled upon an episode of Gruen or drifted into the world of marketing and advertising.

I could have used the word 'reputation'. But brand equity is more than just reputation.

If I was writing this book in 2020, I would still have talked about brand equity. But with the infiltration of artificial intelligence into legal practice and its rapid advancements, the concept of brand equity is more than just what you need to be a successful and contented lawyer. If you do not have brand equity, you may not even become or remain a lawyer. Or at least a lawyer who makes a decent living and is content with their lot in life.

Artificial intelligence is going to take away substantial parts of legal practice which are repetitive and streamlined. Real estate contracts, wills, leases and routine litigation documents, to name a few, will have artificial intelligence produce at least a decent first draft.If you are a senior lawyer, you might still have a job checking that these initial drafts make sense and that artificial intelligence has not hallucinated. But there will be many members of the profession, and regrettably younger members of the profession who will not survive the onslaught of artificial intelligence.

Against that background, your brand equity is your key to survival as a lawyer.

What do I mean by brand equity?

Lawyers have always got work through their reputation, whether internally in their firms or from clients. When I started legal practice, this was the overwhelming way that work was obtained by law firms. For the most part, unless you were well connected at the big end of town, you did the work for a client, did it well, and waited for that client to refer someone to you. It was a slow and painstaking way to build a legal practice.

The 1980s saw, at least in Australia, the growth of multistate law firms and international law firms coming to Australia and establishing their presence here. This trend has not abated. These firms and of course many smaller ones adopted a pyramid structure where there were relatively few owners of the practice and lots of employees generating fees. The overheads of running a legal practice increased enormously.

That structure is hungry for fees which means that in turn it is hungry for work and relying solely on reputation to get work in the door was never going to cut it long term.

This led to very significant marketing efforts initially by the larger firms and then with a trickledown effect to all legal firms including sole practitioners. These marketing efforts are often delivered towards building a brand and reputation for the firm.

Law firms delude themselves that they are building a brand for the firm. What is happening is that they are the beneficiaries of a group of lawyers building individual brands in a particular practice area. The proof of this is when law firms recruit or head hunt a team from another law firm in a practice area. If it was the law firm that had the brand equity, what difference does it make if the lawyers move to another firm? If it was the law firm that had the brand equity, why have restraints of trade in employment agreements or partnership agreements about working for clients in that practice area if you leave the firm?

The brutal reality is that it is the individual lawyers who have the brand equity. However, many lawyers, and particularly young lawyers do not recognise this. Once a lawyer recognises that they have brand equity, they have considerable power in the relationship with the law firm as a partner or an employee.

Much of this book is about building brand equity. Contentment comes from having the power and control in the one person that can use that power and control - you.

Whilst law firms may delude themselves that they are building brand equity in the firm, they are not stupid.

Law firms have become very adept at keeping young lawyers away from clients and away from the community so that they cannot build individual brand equity. Law firms inherently recognise individual brand equity and do what they can to restrict that until it suits the law firm to develop that brand equity as part of the firm's brand.

There are readers of this book who are saying quietly to themselves that they have been practising for several years and never get the chance to speak to a client either by telephone or face-to-face. Their interactions with other law firms are restricted to the mundane. If you are in that position, just how do you build brand equity?

The same way that you became a lawyer in the first place. You must invest in yourself.

You invested in yourself when you incurred a substantial HECS debt to get the law degree. You invested in yourself when you did the practical legal training course.

This means that if the firm is keeping you in a box and not letting you develop your brand as a lawyer then you must spend your hardearned money on that development. It should at least be tax deductible!

Once you have spent a few years in legal practice, you should be starting to work out what areas of legal practice interest you. Hopefully, it is the area in which you are working but it may not be.

We must all do continuing legal education as a condition of maintaining our practising certificates. Go to the seminars or workshops in the area that interests you. If you can, attend a face-to-face seminar rather than online. You will end up meeting other lawyers who are interested in the area. You will be able to have a chat to the speaker, who in theory should know what he or she is talking about in the area. Who knows where all this interaction might lead?

At its most fundamental, knowledge is the foundation upon which you can build your brand equity. No client is going to give you work, and no one is going to refer a client to you if you do not know what you are talking about. You do not have to know everything, but you must know the fundamental issues and law in that practice area.

Practice areas do not exist in isolation. Industry bodies exist to promote the interests of its members. And guess what? Those members are your clients or prospective clients! Every industry body of any size has committees. Inevitably, those committees deal with legal issues. Lawyers are welcome on those committees.

So, to build your brand equity, join an industry body, go to its functions, get on a committee, attend committee meetings, and do the work. If your law firm is prepared to pay for this - great. If it is not, then invest in yourself by paying the membership fee and getting involved.

Another way to build brand equity if you are being kept in a box is to attend conferences of the industry - not legal conferences. Again, you will have to pay for this out of your pocket, and they are generally not cheap when you consider accommodation and airfares. You might also have to use some of your annual leave to do this. You can see how committed you must be to building your brand equity when it is your money and time on the line.

Conversely, don't spread the butter too thinly across the bread. Do not become a member of too many organisations. If you do, you cannot devote the time to fostering the relationships that you will need to build your brand equity.

To put this into context, I will relate my own experience. I was fortunate that my law firms were prepared to invest the money and time in building my brand equity, and which in turn became the firm's brand equity for as long as I remained at the firm.

In the mid 1990s, I started acting for a substantial retirement living and aged care operator. I got involved because one of the partners of my firm was too busy to do their work and asked me to help. I knew absolutely nothing about the sector. However, the initial work drew on my existing commercial and property experience which made it easy to deliver an excellent job very promptly to the client.

There were virtually no legal resources available to learn about the relevant law and indeed even resources about the sector itself were thin on the ground. Nevertheless, I found the sector interesting and started to get hold of what resources I could lay my hands on. I read the relevant legislation. I read a couple of government reports on the sector. The client continued to send me work and I learnt on the job.

After I had gained enough knowledge so that I would not look like a complete idiot amongst industry peers, I joined two industry associations which had the bulk of the clients in the sector as members. In fact, there were another two much smaller industry associations that I did not join as it would have been too expensive, and I was going to spread my butter too thinly.

I got on to a couple of committees. I attended the meetings. I did the work expected of me. Nothing destroys your brand equity more than (on a regular basis) not turning up to committee meetings. Or saying nothing or being unprepared if you do turn up. This is your opportunity to shine. I have been on committees where there have been other lawyers who have quietly destroyed their brand equity by doing exactly what I have said you should not do.

It was not long before other committee members were sending me work. I was learning about the sector and about the issues that confronted the sector. I put my hand up to do some presentations at workshops and at conferences.

I started attending conferences. Members of the committees that I was on were happy to introduce me at the conferences to other people that they knew in the sector both locally and interstate. I honed my networking skills.

There was a considerable amount of time outside of billable time that I had to put into these activities. And it took years. It paid off in spades.

One of the nicest compliments that I ever received in legal practice was when the CEO of one of the retirement living and aged care clients told me that the sector did not consider me as their lawyer but as *'one of them'*.

My brand equity was such that the practice expanded from me with one client to several lawyers working almost exclusively for that sector. But when I left that firm, my brand equity followed me to my new firm. So did the clients.

The point of that anecdote is to illustrate how much time, effort and money you must throw at something to get the return on equity. If your law firm is prepared to do that, pay them the respect that they deserve. They should also get a return on their investment. If you are content at that firm, stay there. Even if you are not content stay there long enough to repay the firm's effort in developing your brand equity. Then it is a win win for you and the firm. But if you are not content at that firm, you have built your own brand equity, and as my anecdote shows, it follows you. Clients follow your brand equity.

If your firm is not prepared to assist you, and you have invested the time, effort and money, then you owe the law firm nothing and can move on to where you will be content and respected for your brand equity.

But brand equity is not just a set and forget exercise. It requires you to keep up with the law, keep up with the issues that confront the relevant industry and it requires you to understand all of that. But in the context of artificial intelligence, lawyers who have developed deep brand equity will still be required by business or by individuals who require knowledge, expertise and judgement. In a world where artificial intelligence will eventually commoditise a lot of legal practice, these three things will become more valuable. You have them and your clients want to pay for them.

There is an excellent book on legal practice management written a couple of decades ago by David Maister called *The Trusted Advisor*. Never have those words been more relevant. In the world of artificial intelligence, lawyers who ascribe to being a trusted advisor will be more content and successful than those that do not.

10

The 4As

Following the 4As is not a guarantee for contentment or success or both. But it will go a long way towards that goal.

In order of importance, the 4As are:

- Ability
- Affability
- Availability
- Affordability

These are your characteristics which will hold you in good stead as you progress through the legal profession.

But these are just words, and they need some definition and context. Let's look at each one of them in turn.

Ability

I have mentioned before that your ability as a lawyer is critical to your contentment and success. We all have differing levels of ability and the legal profession is very good at sorting out the wheat from the chaff. Like every profession, we need stars who become leaders and have the intellect and the work ethic to expand the law and its benefits for society. But not everyone can be at that standard or wants or needs to be.

Lawyers do need to ask the hard question of whether they have the ability to practice in a particular area of law, both in the knowledge of the law but also in dealing with the type of clients that need expertise in that area. Occasionally, I have come across lawyers who have never asked this question of themselves!

If you know your ability and what you are capable of, it gives you the confidence to give the advice to the clients and attract clients who need your services. You should challenge yourself with a more difficult area of law or even more difficult cases within your chosen speciality. But do not bite off more than you can chew. Clients expect that you are competent and will, quite rightly, hold you to that standard. If you have the ability to meet that standard, then your stress levels remain at an acceptable level.

Importantly, ability attracts clients. Clients refer other clients to you because you can do the job. It helps you to earn a decent living.

Affability

We are in the people business. Lawyers who can easily relate to clients attract clients. Lawyers who can easily relate to other lawyers attract respect and referrals. Lawyers who can easily relate to administrative and managerial staff attract both respect and support.

The legal profession is littered with difficult and often cantankerous lawyers. I suspect that the pressures of legal practice exacerbate preexisting psychological tendencies to exhibit these behaviours.

For some lawyers, this type of personality suits certain clients and certain areas of law. But they are the exception rather than the rule.

What I do know is that clients, staff and other lawyers much prefer dealing with affable lawyers. By affable, I do not mean that you walk around the office with a permanent smile on your face, laughing and cracking jokes.

By affable, I mean that you are sufficiently interested in life that you are able to hold a conversation with people from all walks of life and make them feel as if they matter in your life.

Affability does not mean that you can't ask the challenging questions. That is your job. But it is the way that you ask challenging questions that matters.

It is human nature to be attracted to people to whom you can relate. When you are purchasing professional services such as engaging an accountant or going to the dentist, surely you prefer dealing with someone that you can relate to rather than someone who has the personality of a wet lettuce leaf?

Availability

From reading the previous chapters of this book you would be surprised that this A has made the list.

Being available as a lawyer to your clients, staff, other lawyers and the courts and external bureaucracy and so on does not mean that you are switched on 24/7.

But it does mean that when you are '*lawyering,*' you are available to do the job that you are getting paid for.

I am constantly surprised at how many lawyers do not understand this fundamental principle. We have all experienced the frustration of other lawyers who do not return phone calls and do not answer emails or correspondence. So, imagine what it must feel like if your client cannot get a response from you during the hours when you profess that you are practising as a lawyer?

This does not mean that you take every phone call, answer emails instantly and so on. There are times in the law when you just have to focus on the task at hand and block out all of the noise. In those circumstances, it is appropriate to put '*do not disturb*' on the telephone, shut the door and get the job done. Once the job is done, become available again.

Affordability

Affordability does not mean cheap. Affordability is matching the value that your ability, affability and availability bring to your client with what your client should pay.

The advent of artificial intelligence on accomplishing routine tasks in the law will change the affordability equation forever.

The routine tasks will be commoditised and charged at a rate which reflects the use of artificial intelligence.

It will bring into sharp focus the affordability of your legal services which artificial intelligence, at least at this stage, cannot replicate. Following the other 3As will enable you to price those legal services to reflect the value that your skills bring to solving your clients' legal problems.

This is not a book about how to price your services, although I will lightly touch on these issues in later chapters.

However, a couple of anecdotes will illustrate my above point, even though they are drawn from a time before artificial intelligence impacted the profession.

A property developer client asked me to put in a tender for bulk conveyancing services for a number of its land developments. I did so at a significant discount to standard conveyancing prices given the volume and the synergies that would come from doing repetitive work. I lost the tender. It was the second or third tender that I had lost on providing conveyancing services for this client. I had a good relationship with the general manager of the client and did quite a bit of high level property development legal advice for the client.

I rang up the general manager and asked him why I had lost the tender and why I kept losing these tenders. He told me that the tender had been won by another legal firm at about 50% of what I was prepared to charge. He told me that my competitor had simply bought the work in order to get access to the better quality property development work. He said it was not a question of competency as they only put out a request for tender to firms that could do the work. He said it was simply a numbers game and going with the other firm added dollars to the bottom line of his business. It made his job easier when it came to budget time.

And that was before artificial intelligence!

A few years later, my firm received a request for tender from a client in an industry where my firm did the work for the majority of businesses in the industry. The unusual thing about this request for tender was that it specified that my firm could only charge the hourly rate specified in the tender, which happened to be about 80% of what we were charging everybody else.

As politely as we could, we wrote to the client and informed them that we would not be prepared to tender on that basis. The reason was that if we gave them that deal, every other client would find out because of the closeknit nature of the industry and demand the same deal. We would have wiped 20% off of our gross revenue and in reality about 66% of our profit. We knew our value to the industry, and we were prepared to walk away from a client to preserve that value.

The irony of that anecdote is that the firm that did win the tender did not have the expertise in a critical area, and after finding that out, the client began to instruct us again - at the correct hourly rate.

So why does following the 4As matter as far as being a contented lawyer is concerned? Because they underpin the techniques which enable you to survive and prosper in legal practice.

The remainder of this book is about those techniques.

11

The art of communication

The law is like a gigantic jigsaw puzzle without a border. Some pieces were installed centuries ago. Over the centuries the rough edges of these pieces were smoothed over. As society grew and became more complex, more pieces were added to the jigsaw and most of them do not fit neatly. You have to push them into place and hope they don't dislodge the piece next to them. Courts and Parliament keep throwing more pieces into the jigsaw and sometimes taking them away.

Lawyers have a special gift. They can look at the jigsaw puzzle and work out how it fits together and where it doesn't fit together. They get this special gift by going to Law School and then entering the legal profession. Bit by bit they are given pieces of the jigsaw to work out how they all fit.

Our clients do not have this gift. They come to us and

ask us to use this gift to help them.

For centuries, lawyers did their best to keep this gift under wraps. Only those in society who became lawyers got to untie the ribbon and unwrap the gift. The method they used to do this was called legalese.

It is a special type of language using a mixture of Latin and arcane English designed to prevent otherwise intelligent and sometimes not so intelligent people from understanding how the jigsaw fits together and how it might help them.

But in all the centuries, the role of the lawyer never changed. Their role was to use the gift to understand the law, interpret the law and communicate to our clients how that law could resolve the client's problem. The art of communication lies at the essence of what we do as lawyers.

The legal profession has got better at the art of communication, but there is still a long way to go. In the context of this book, excelling at the art of communication helps you become a contented lawyer.

Let me explain with an anecdote.

The first 10 years or so of my practising career were spent primarily in litigation. Although litigation was not immune to legalese, the necessity to plead your client's case and match the individual facts of your case to the law, meant that there was some logic and some logical order applied to the preparation of correspondence and documents. On top of that, the opposing side applied pressure to make sure that you made it very clear what your client's position was. And that was before the judiciary got involved!

As my commercial practice developed, the contrast with commercial documents was stark. As it happened, I started preparing and reviewing lots of leases and trust documents. They were dense and almost impenetrable. Sentences would consist of hundreds of words without punctuation. The use of Latin was commonplace. New concepts were simply added at the back of the document with no connection to other clauses dealing with a related issue. It was like a hundred-year-old soup to which new words had been added and stirred in without any thought as to how that would taste: either to lawyers or to their clients.

Just when I thought that I would rather be stabbed through the eye with a compass needle than read another 60 page lease filled with legalese, I came across a book called *Plain Language for Lawyers* by Michele Asprey. It was not a long book and I read it in one sitting on an airline flight.

It was an epiphany. The author showed the stupidity of using legalese and more importantly showed various techniques on how to do away with this approach and prepare documents that people could understand.

I read other publications and books on the same theme. I practised what was preached. I even went back to university to do a course on plain language.

As the course lecturer said: "*Make every word earn its keep.*"

It made me an inherently better communicator because I had to read the legalese, use these techniques to take it apart and produce correspondence and documents that people could understand. I became the filter through which complex laws and complex facts could be communicated in understandable language to clients for their benefit.

I took this approach to oral advice as well.

There was strong resistance at the time (in the early 1990s) from many sections of the profession. But 35 years on, the battle has been well and truly won by those wishing to use plain language. Indeed, and somewhat ironically, legislation in many areas makes it the law to do so. Lawyers ignore this at their peril.

But what has all this got to do with the theme of this book? Principally, because the clients love it. It makes their life easier in so many ways, particularly if those documents are standard form documents which the client then has to use in the marketplace to generate business for itself.

I have lost count of the number of clients who instructed me because of the use of plain language in my drafting and communication. It was the ability to communicate the complexity of the law in a way that clients could understand that drew in the clients.

It was a telling illustration of two of the 4As, namely ability and affability.

And in a way, it was also an illustration of affordability as clients were prepared to pay a premium for documents that they and their customers could understand. One client said that the conversion of a retirement village contract to a plain language one had been very successful with the customers of the client. Consequently, they were able to deploy a staff member elsewhere whose sole job had been to go through the legalese document. It saved the client money and my reward for that was more work from the client.

Writing in plain language takes considerable skill and discipline. But at least you get the chance to review the document you have produced and tinker with it.

But when you are advising your client face-to-face, on the telephone, in a video conference or in front of the judiciary, you do not have that luxury. You need to be able to communicate *'on-the-fly.'*

Modern legal practice has diminished the ability of lawyers to be able to communicate *'on-the-fly.'* When I started practice, apart from writing letters you communicated with clients in meetings and on the telephone. Busy practitioners would have several meetings a day and having 20 phone calls a day was by no means unusual.

Compare that to modern day practice when instructions come in by email, and the lawyer gives the advice by email. Meetings, telephone calls and videoconferences are the exception rather than the rule.

In a world where people would rather send someone a text than get on the telephone and have a chat, the art of verbal communication is under pressure.

When I was discussing this with a junior lawyer

in my office, she made the comment that she was not comfortable giving advice on the telephone without having the time to think about whether she was right or wrong. She said that some of her colleagues in large firms had never spoken to a client despite having been in practice for several years!

I was a bit taken aback by this conversation and reflected back on my junior lawyer days. The reason I was comfortable giving advice to the client on the telephone was that I had sat through countless telephone conversations where one of the senior lawyers in my first firm was advising a client. The reason I had sat through those countless telephone conversations was that the senior lawyer was constantly on the phone. I knew that the only way to get a word in was in between these conversations. What I didn't realise at the time was that through osmosis, I was learning how to give advice and communicate to the client.

I learned how to listen. I learned how to push back. I learned how to say that I could not give an answer to that straight away and that I would get back to the client. I learned how to give hard advice that the client did not wish to hear.

I am forever grateful for that training.

Regrettably, the opportunities to gain experience this way are getting less for junior lawyers. But if the opportunity does come up to sit in on a meeting with a senior colleague or listen to that colleague dispense advice on the telephone: take it, even if you might have to stay back for half an hour to get your billable time up.

The art of communication is one of the most useful skills that you can ever learn as a lawyer. If you get good at it, you get satisfied clients, you get more clients, you have better relationships within your firm, you do better in litigation and so on.

Too often, lawyers are keen to show their knowledge of the law by writing letters and emails as if they are making a submission to the High Court. They speak using words and terminology only other lawyers would understand. I have seen countless examples where the written advice is footnoted with case references and the legal citation for the case. As if the client would give a stuff - let alone understand the legal citation. Clients aren't interested in you showing that you know the law. They have assumed that when they hired you. What they are interested in is a solution to their problem in language that they can understand.

By the way, if you want your advice to have the footnotes and the legal citation for future reference, do that in the first draft and then get rid of it for the one that goes to the client!

It is a good illustration of the adage of '*the law is 50% know and 50% show*.' Knowledge of the law is pretty useless if you cannot show how that knowledge can help the client.

Part of the art of communication is the ability to communicate at the level that the client requires for proper comprehension of your advice. If you are giving advice to a CEO who has a law degree and an accounting degree, even if you write in plain language or speak plainly, you can pitch your advice at a more complex level. There is no point in doing that with a person who has a personal injury claim, has never spoken to a lawyer in their life and is dyslexic.

It takes time to master this subtlety in communication. One way to see if you are mastering this skill is after you have given the advice to the client, ask the client to express in their own words the essence of what you have just said. It is a bit like sitting for an exam and getting instantly marked on your performance.

When I have done this with clients that I sense are struggling with what I am trying to say to them, I have been quite surprised at what they thought I was saying. You might then have to approach it in a different way to get the message across.

A good technique is to give the advice in small blocks and then ask a question which requires the client to have understood the advice to give a suitable response. If the client cannot give a suitable response, you know you have a problem and you have to go back and revisit the issue.

I could go on about the various techniques necessary to achieve this, but there are many books available that can teach you these techniques. Read them. Use them. Get better with practice.

You can test yourself after every email, letter or document that you prepare on Microsoft Word and in Microsoft Outlook. In Microsoft Word, under the 'Home' tab, click on 'Editor' in the ribbon and it will come up with an analysis of your writing and make suggestions for corrections. Once you have gone through all of that, under 'Insights', you can click on 'Document stats', and it will break down the document into some key metrics for plain language. Under the readability section, it will tell you how easy the document is to read (the higher the score the easier it is) and what educational level you need to have achieved to understand the document.

This book has been written so that a person with a year 8 level of education can read it and understand it. In other words, a 13 year old should have no problem with it.

Earlier in this chapter I reflected on the words of my lecturer who implored me '*to make every word earn its keep*.' What he meant by that was to only use as many words as necessary to communicate properly and not pad out the advice.

But I recognise that in some firms, you do not get the freedom to do this. Some lawyers have different views than me and if you want to keep your job you need to adhere to those views.

Conversely, if you work for someone like me then if you want to keep your job you have to adhere to those views on plain language and communication!

Some years ago, I had spent about three years training a junior lawyer on how to communicate in plain language. He had mastered the techniques quite well.

He then decided to seek greener pastures in a different practice area with a major Australia wide law firm.

About a year later I ran into him in the street and asked how he was going. He said that he was working for a partner who had asked him to prepare a letter of advice to an insurance company client about the prospects of defending a claim. The lawyer had said that he had followed my plain language techniques that I had taught him and had distilled the advice into a couple of pages. When he presented that to the partner, he was met with a response that the advice was correct, but it was not long enough and would never justify the fee that he wanted to charge the client. He was told to go and make the advice at least seven or eight pages long!

You can't win them all.

And when you are communicating with clients, your colleagues in the legal profession, the bureaucracy, the court system and so on - keep it respectful. Sometimes you have to give forthright advice or rebut or make allegations which mean you have to employ clear and unequivocal language.

If you have to write that sort of email or letter, and you have the time, leave it in the draft box overnight and read it again with a fresh mind in the morning. More often than not, when I have done that, the email or letter gets amended. If it is a borderline letter, get a colleague to read it through who is not afraid to tell you that you have got it wrong.

A good baseline is to follow the advice given to me as a young lawyer by a colleague in my firm. He said: "*Only write a letter that you are prepared to sit in the witness box in the Supreme Court and get crossexamined on.*"

12

The art of business development

No matter how big a law firm is, the revenue side of the profit and loss account comes down to three principles. Get the work, do the work and get paid for the work - in that order!

If you do that you and you price your services correctly and match your overheads to the type of law firm you are running, then you will make a decent living.

In this chapter, I will focus on the first principle - getting the work.

Getting work in the legal profession has become more challenging over the decades since I started practice. This is not particularly surprising because the number of lawyers has expanded exponentially since that time. When I was admitted as a lawyer in South Australia in 1978, I was allocated number 1492 in the Roll of Practitioners which meant that only 1491 lawyers had preceded me since the numbered system commenced in 1920. I have searched the records from colonisation of South Australia in 1836 and there are about 300 lawyers admitted from then until 1920. So there were not many of us around when I started out!

At that time, Law Schools only existed in the major universities in each capital city in Australia. Universities quickly worked out that Law Schools were relatively cheap to run and they could charge good fees for law degrees. Before long, every university had a Law School and they churn out thousands of potential lawyers every year.

Therefore, compared to some professions there are many more places available at university to study law. But because of the sheer number of graduates from law, it is incredibly competitive to obtain a position in a law firm. Once you are in the profession, there are only lightweight restrictive trade practices to meet to enable you to advance in the profession.

We have all had the same fundamental training to enable us to get our practising certificate. In that sense, we enter the profession on a relatively even playing field. The ability to develop your business and find work to do is an important differentiator in the profession. How you deal with that differentiation underpins how contented you can be as a lawyer.

For the most part, the traditional areas of legal practice are much the same as they have always been. Thankfully, governments can't help themselves and keep expanding the laws and their complexity (in traditional areas and new areas), giving our profession an ever expanding smorgasbord of potential work.

Little wonder that if you are going to work in the traditional areas of legal practice, you will find it awash with competitors. It is challenging to differentiate yourself from your competitors. If that area is awash with work, then you will survive because of that. But if that work is unprofitable or barely profitable because of the competition, what is the point? If that area relies on continued government legislation supporting the area, what happens if that support is removed or curtailed?

It is a fundamental rule of business that if you can limit your competitors, you can more easily develop your business and be more profitable.

One of my favourite sayings is: *'If you don't want competition, practice in an area that is difficult.'*

Why do you think it is that taxation lawyers are relatively thin upon the ground and can charge a premium rate for their services?

I have had personal experience of this principle. For about the last 25 years of my career, I practised in succession law and in what I would call housing and accommodation law covering housing developments, retirement villages, aged care and similar accommodation concepts.

In succession law, it was challenging to implement business development techniques to be heard above the noise of the significant competition from the many practitioners in this area. Thankfully, the sheer amount of work coming from an ageing population meant that there was still a sufficient flow of work.

But in the housing and accommodation law area, the complexity of the regulatory environment proved a barrier to competitors. Although it took a lot of effort to keep up with the law (which changed with regularity), business development was significantly easier because there were fewer competitors, or at least competitors who were prepared to put in the hard yards to show their ability to the clients.

But you should not choose a difficult area which does not align with what you are interested in as a lawyer. Because the area is difficult, you will need passion and discipline to stay the course. If you do, the reward is less competition for clients and you can implement some of the following business development strategies.

One of my colleagues used to say that: "*Every law firm partnership consisted of finders, minders and grinders.*" By that he meant that the finders found the work and the clients, the minders kept the clients that had been found and the grinders churned out the fees for the clients that the finders had found and that the minders had kept.

He was right to say that every law firm partnership did consist of finders, minders and grinders. The real question is whether they should.

In one sense, every lawyer is a finder, minder and grinder. Every lawyer has these attributes in varying quantities. These quantities vary over time.

Every lawyer should ask themselves what is the appropriate percentage that they have of these attributes. For example, a lawyer who is primarily a grinder finds it incredibly stressful and difficult to become a finder. I have seen lawyers whose ability as a grinder sees them beating budget every year and upon appointment as a partner they suddenly realise that this is not enough and you have to be a finder and a minder as well. The pressure from other partners to deliver on those attributes can cause considerable stress.

Conversely, I have seen lawyers who are primarily finders become stressed when asked to grind away and meet budget consistently. "*But look at all the work I bring in*" they usually say at the annual budget meeting to a bunch of stony-faced colleagues. Those colleagues secretly resent the finder being away at a conference for three days whilst they are grinding away meeting budget and keeping the cash coming in.

You can see that being a square peg smashed into a round hole can cause significant stress and lack of contentment in a lawyer.

Within law firms, the necessity to be a finder diminishes as the law firm grows in size. A sole practitioner has to be a finder, otherwise he or she will be staring at a blank screen every day. In small to medium size firms where the relationship between the client and the lawyer is very strong and where repeat business is critical, the finder is a prized member of the firm. Once you get into the bigger firms, the ability to grind out the work at pace and at a premium price are highly valued.

Nevertheless, even the large legal firms need a preponderance of finders at partnership level.

Because if you cannot find the work, the other two types of lawyers become irrelevant. There is no reason for their existence.

That is why this chapter focuses on the art of business development and becoming a finder. Deep down, law firms know that the finders are the key to a successful law firm. Law firms, certainly at a senior level, recruit lawyers with a proven ability to find and attract clients. Law firms know that they can buy grinders and they can keep the minders happy with interesting clients, work and a decent salary.

In short, finders are the ones usually sought after by firms and the ones who are likely to command a premium income. That is why you should at least read the rest of this chapter and if finding work is within your skill set, you might apply some of my thoughts to your practice.

The art of business development justifies its own book. There are many books that have been written on that topic for lawyers and professionals generally. You could do worse than reading one or two of these books and gleaning techniques which you could apply to your practice area.

After about 10 years in legal practice, I read a book by an American lawyer called Jay Foonberg called '*How to start and build a law practice*'. Although it was written through the eyes of the American legal system as it was in the 1980s, it contained a lot of very useful techniques and thoughts. The sixth edition of the book was published in 2020 and is still available.

And so, whilst the fine grain of business development always changes, there are some fundamental principles that never do. They are as relevant now as they were when I read Foonberg. When I read that book, the Internet only existed between the major universities in the world, social media did not exist and any mobile phones were the size of a briefcase.

It is trite to say that we live in a vastly different world. But here are some relevant principles to develop your business as a lawyer which have not changed dramatically since I read that book.

Let's assume that you have nailed the 4As. Business development is getting clients to know that you have nailed them.

You could sit in your office and wait for the work to come to you. But finder is the term given to the lawyer, not the client.

Therefore, you have to put yourself before clients or where the clients might be. That does require some due diligence on who are the clients and where they might be.

Let's not talk in the abstract. Say that you want to work for property developers. The first question that you might want to ask is what type of property development work you want to do. Property developers do work ranging from master planned land divisions, through to complex apartment buildings, commercial buildings with multiple tenancies, community housing and so on.

If you try to be all things to all property developers, you will spread the butter too thinly across the bread.

Instead, focus on one area within the property development industry. The skills to put together a complex apartment building in the middle of the city are different to the skills needed to achieve broad acre land division. They may well be underpinned by the same fundamental knowledge of property law, but there are significant differences between the two. And sometimes, property developers who do apartment buildings never want to touch a broad acre land division and the other way around. An experienced property lawyer could do both. But if you are starting out, you are better to focus on one area.

Let's say that you have decided to focus on the community housing sector which does a lot of property development work. A few simple Internet searches and you will quickly find out who are the clients available to you. Assuming that there are enough to make it worth your effort, how are you going to contact these clients?

The fundamental way is to go where these clients gather. Inevitably, they have an industry lobby organisation. Join it. Get involved with it by sitting on committees or even on the board. Go to functions organised by the organisation.

You will need to use your affability, but getting involved with the organisation means that you can subtly display your skills in committee meetings and general discussions with the clients.

The other place they gather is at conferences. Even if you go to a conference and do not meet or speak to any clients, you will be listening to what is concerning the industry. You are getting '*in the tent*' with the industry.

You then have the chance to build on that by communicating that ability to the industry at large. Clients do not care about newsletters or podcasts unless there is something in it for them. Then, they are very interested in getting essentially free legal advice or knowledge that they can use in their business.

By now you should know who are the clients in the industry and how to communicate with them, by email, by inviting them to follow you on social media, by podcasts and so on.

Consistency is the key in this communication strategy. Sending out an annual newsletter will not cut it.

This consistency was highlighted to me when the CEO of a major aged care organisation said that his inbox had plenty of newsletters coming from law firms going on about this and that. He said he deleted them as they were coming in except for one. He said that was the one from one of my colleagues who was developing her workplace relations practice in the aged care sector. Every two or three weeks, she would find an interesting case in workplace relations and write a punchy onepage summary with some advice as to what that case meant for risk management in that area. The CEO said that he always read that newsletter. He recognised that this was a real benefit to him running his business.

What if my colleague had only done this every three or four months when she '*had the time*'? I suspect it would have ended up getting deleted like all the other ones. It took time and effort from my colleague to be consistent but it reaped the reward of that organisation sending workplace relations work from its previous firm to my colleague.

Another important way of communicating your ability to your chosen industry is to give presentations to that industry. You can do this through presentations at conferences for that industry, although in recent years this has become more difficult as law firms which become sponsors of conferences insist on one of their lawyers giving the presentation and blocking the competition. Fair enough. You have to get something back for your sponsorship dollars.

If that happens, do your own presentation at your own conference for that industry. This is particularly useful if you have a substantial topic, such as a change in legislation to work through. In some ways these presentations are even better because you get to control the narrative, the setting and interaction with clients.

But this attraction of clients and work does not happen overnight. There is no hard and fast rule about how long it takes. Nevertheless, I have the three year rule. If you follow the above approach for a particular industry for three years and you cannot pinpoint one client that has come to you through those efforts, acknowledge that it has failed and try something else or try another industry. If you have got a couple of clients through this method, assess whether it is worth continuing the effort or focusing on something else.

I have tried this approach on several industries (and there are many techniques which underpin that approach) and it has worked successfully except for once.

Many years ago, I decided to try to get more complex estate planning work from private clients. I was getting a few referrals from financial planners who had encouraged me to do some presentations at industry seminars and seminars for the financial planning groups and so on. I did so for several years, and the feedback was always very positive.

But the clients and the increase in referrals didn't come. Maybe they were lying to me in relation to the feedback! The real reason was that it was not up to the financial planner to send me the work. They had to convince their client to use me in preference to their existing lawyer, or indeed to do some estate planning in the first place.

It was not the financial planners at fault. It was me. I had not done my due diligence on the referrers and the potential for more clients. I should have asked the referrers who were enticing me to give the presentations to outline what steps were needed before they could refer a client for estate planning and what had been the conversion rate in the past.

In any event, after three years of failure, I resisted every subsequent invitation to do a presentation to financial planners and their clients. I put my efforts elsewhere.

I have gone into this approach in detail because that is the entry point to the clients. But the art is called '*business development*' for a reason. Once you have gotten through the front door, you then have to develop the business that is laid out before you. This is where some of the soft techniques such as attending industry lunches, organising inhouse lunches, catching up with clients for a coffee and so on come to the fore.

But I have seen too many lawyers place too much emphasis on these techniques and get disappointed when they do not seem to work. Good clients are busy people - otherwise why do you want their business? An hour spent with you having a chat over coffee is an hour away from their business. Are you really happy to spend an hour of your time having a chat to the business which supplies your photocopiers? Probably not, unless you are about to buy a photocopier.

And it is the same for our clients. Give them a reason to come out for a coffee or for lunch. It might be that you have come across something that might be useful for your client's business. It might be an introduction to someone that your client should meet. Too often, networking is seen by lawyers as the lawyer being at the centre of the wheel with the spokes going out to all of the clients and that is the sum total of the network. Networking is far more than that. It is the tyre rim to which the spokes are connected and the crisscrossing of spokes between the people in your network which delivers benefit to your client, and ultimately to you in more work.

When you get a client, don't move onto the next one. It is disrespectful to the client. The art is to develop business from the client that has decided to use you. This is an easier task than constantly seeking new clients. You do not have to prove yourself over and over again. That's where minding and grinding can assist. It is also a way to sell more services of your firm to that client. But only if you follow the 4As!

I have seen examples of law firms which bombarded existing clients (who also happened to be my clients) with capability statements, newsletters and so on about other expertise in the law firm. Clients are not stupid. The reason that they have decided to use you is because of you following the 4As! It is also probably the reason why they use another law firm for different expertise. In a subtle way, telling them why they should use you instead of a law firm that they are happy with, is telling your prospective client that they do not know what they are doing in selecting legal firms!

A good rule to follow is to not prise a client away from another law firm with which they are happy. By all means, continue to gently promote your firm's expertise and your expertise (as the case may be) so that if a conflict of interest arises or the relationship sours, the client knows where to come for expertise and assistance.

But think deeply about how much of your precious resources you are going to devote to that task.

I'll give you a real-life example. I had developed a retirement village and aged care practice to the point where the majority of clients in that sector in my State used me and my firm for much of their legal work. Many of those clients also used another firm for similar legal work and also for work for which the other firm had particular expertise. There were some clients in that sector who exclusively used me and some who exclusively used the other firm.

The nature of the industry was that everybody knew everybody else and I knew that the clients who used the other firm were happy with that firm. Nevertheless, I got to know one particular client through one of its senior managers being on a committee with me and I would cross paths with other managers of that business at conferences and so on. But I never pitched for their work.

But the client got to know about my four A's through meeting me and talking to my other clients in the sector. Eventually, the client did contact me for advice about an issue where the client thought that my expertise was deeper than the other firm. After that, I got more work from the client which still used the other firm for the overwhelming majority of its work.

Business development is often about deciding where to allocate resources. You cannot do everything. The old adage of getting *'bang for your buck'* applies very much to business development. Do not waste precious resources chasing work and clients that you have little hope of winning.

It is another way of saying that you need to do due diligence on clients and potential work before starting to chase it. Commercial lawyers are very familiar with the concept of due diligence particularly when a client is acquiring another business. Clients do not part with their money unless they have done a '*deep dive*' into the underlying business that they are acquiring. But how often do lawyers throw huge amounts of marketing resources at prospective clients or a prospective industry without having done the due diligence on whether they can genuinely acquire the work?

The above approach is a good one for attracting work from clients who have an ongoing need for lawyers and one client can generate many matters. But there is a vast amount of legal work where clients will use a lawyer on one occasion, such as family law, personal injury claims or criminal law. Very often this is the province of sole practitioners and small firms.

These clients are likely to find a lawyer by asking someone if they know a good lawyer who could help them with getting a divorce, sorting out a criminal charge and so on.

The key to that sentence is '*asking someone*'. Your key to getting that work is to have that someone be part of your referral network. Of course, that may be an existing or past client that you have done a good job for and who refers a friend or relative to you for a similar job.

But equally, it could be a referrer who knows about you by other means. Accounting firms are good referrers. A client of an accounting firm goes back every year to get their accounts done and if they have a legal problem such as a family law problem, they will often involve their accountant and often ask for a referral to '*someone good*'. So, if you want to get accountants to refer you family law work, why aren't you presenting to groups of accountants on that topic? It does not have to be to one of the professional bodies of the accounting profession. Existing accounting clients of the firm will do just fine.

Other lawyers are great referrers of work. But they will only do so if they have great faith in your ability and you do not steal the client for other legal work. It is quite easy to show your ability to other lawyers by giving presentations at the Law Society or other CPD providers or writing articles in Law Society publications. In some areas of law such as estate litigation, where multiple parties have to be independently represented, other lawyers involved in the dispute will often refer un-represented people to good lawyers. You get that type of work by following the 4As. No lawyer wants to refer a client to another lawyer and then get the referred client complaining about level of service, ability and so on.

Over the years, after doing a job for a client referred by another lawyer, the client has wanted to retain me to do other work. I have only done so with the consent of the referring lawyer. You breach that rule, and word gets around pretty quickly and you won't get another referral from anyone.

If you get a job referred by an accountant or another lawyer or a former or current client, a quick email or handwritten note to say thanks is imperative. No need to shower them with gifts, but everyone appreciates a thank you.

But you cannot say thank you if you do not know where the referral has come from. Clients will often volunteer that they have been referred by a particular person, but often they are so concerned about the legal problem that they forget. You must not forget. You must ask. Do not die wondering. The answer to that question may lead you to contact someone who turns out to be an excellent referrer of work.

And so, the fundamental message from this chapter is that you have to find a way to promote yourself to your potential clients and in turn the work that they can provide to you. Following the above principles should achieve that. There are many techniques which underpin those principles and some of those you will learn from reading books on business development or attending seminars on the topic. Some you will learn by trying them and succeeding, and some you will learn by trying them and failing. I abide by the adage: '*In the law, nothing that you do is ever wasted.*' You will always learn from it.

What does all this mean in the context of the theme of this book? Fundamentally, you can only be content when who you are matches what you are being asked to do as a lawyer. In the early years, it is difficult to be anything other than a grinder. There is nothing wrong with that as that is where you learn how to draft, how to analyse and how to produce work of an acceptable standard. If that is all you want to do for the rest of your career, that is fine. However, that means that your work life and your income is dictated to by the finders and minders of the firm.

Once the early years are over, you do need to decide whether to become a finder, a minder or a grinder or a combination of all of them and in what proportion. That will give you more control over your work life and your income. You retain the power to use your skills for your benefit. Is that a better place to be than just being a grinder? That is for you to decide, but if you want to be a finder, then hopefully the contents of this chapter are of some use.

13

The art of delegation

Now that you have managed to get work, you need to get it done.

Delegation is the key to this task.

Clients delegate a legal problem to a lawyer. The principles of delegation apply equally to this delegation as they do to a senior partner delegating work to a graduate lawyer.

Private clients rarely know how to properly delegate a legal problem to a lawyer. Commercial clients are better at it, but in my experience still do so at a pretty basic level. The exceptions are inhouse counsel and experienced managerial staff who know that a clear brief to the lawyer means you receive a better quality answer.

From the lawyer's perspective, the fundamental principles are to get a very clear idea of what is the problem, the evidence or resources available within the client's domain to address the problem and the timeline for delivering the answer.

This is one area where advances in technology have made things worse from the lawyer's perspective. When I started practice, apart from the most basic instructions (such as setting up a company or trust or drafting a standard form lease), clients gave you instructions either face-to-face or on the telephone. Lawyers could clarify issues, seek further instructions and work out gaps to be filled before taking on the job. It was by no means perfect, but you had a better chance of making sure that what you were doing was what the client was expecting you to do.

The advent of the fax machine changed this slightly, but in reality, the fax machine was just a way to get a letter sent more quickly than the post.

But the advent of email and the ability to send detailed text messages turned this approach on its ear. Suddenly clients considered it good enough to attach a bunch of documents to an email with a cryptic message such as: "*Can you have a quick look at this and let me know if there are any red flags?*". The risks to lawyers in taking that as complete instructions and giving the fee estimate and getting on with the job are manifest.

I have lost count of the number of times that upon receiving a similar type of email and prodding the client for further information, you uncover relevant documents that the client thought were unnecessary for you to consider, you uncover relevant conversations and so on. Not doing this is akin to a bricklayer being asked to build a brick fence and fix the price without knowing how long the fence is going to be.

So if you don't want to do work that the client does not want you to do (and more importantly pay for) and you could spend the wasted time on other profitable work, do not just accept the delegation without question. It will save a lot of tears in the long run.

When you are starting off in the legal profession, the work is delegated to you. The same principle applies in that as a young lawyer you need to know the scope of what you are being asked to do, what resources are available to you to assist in answering the client's problem and what the timeline is for the delivery of the work.

Although that sounds incredibly simple and when you read it on paper it makes common sense, I have seen a lot of evidence that the legal profession pays lip service to this principle.

I am not a saint in this area, and I am sure that over the years I have breached that principle. The lawyer doing the delegating may be pressed for time, assumes that the lawyer who receives the delegated work has knowledge or skills in excess of what is needed and so on. Fair enough reasons for breaching the principle, but experience tells us that this approach will often end in tears.

It may sound obvious, but taking 10 minutes to properly delegate a job is cheaper than writing off several hours of a junior lawyer's time who has gone '*off piste*' because he or she did not understand what was being asked of them.

Clients do not like paying for work that is of no benefit to them, and sometimes sophisticated clients can easily pick that out in the detailed time entries. Clients also do not like pay for the time taken to do that delegation as they consider that to be an internal cost. Unless you are working on a project where you have told the client at the start that there will need to be a meeting at which the work needs to be divided up amongst a number of lawyers, the clients have a point.

But in the context of getting work done (and having a contented life as a lawyer) why do lawyers have difficulty in delegating work?

Good lawyers have a strong perfectionist streak in them. The law and the legal profession is such a hard taskmaster that you don't survive very long if you do not have that streak within you.

What this does is encourage lawyers to think that only they can do the particular task in front of them. Lawyers know that it will take time to delegate and supervise properly and start thinking: '*I can get it done quicker myself*'. And then thinking: '*I would at least then know that it is done correctly*'.

And the outcome of all that thinking is working longer and longer hours to the detriment of the wellbeing of the lawyer.

The time costing system has imposed, somewhat ironically, a limit on what a lawyer can earn by doing the work themselves. Therefore, at some point every lawyer has to either learn to say no to more work or learn to delegate the work or implement a more efficient way of producing the work within the same amount of time.

Lawyers are notorious for never refusing work which is within their field of competence. For some reason, it is ingrained into our DNA at an early stage that if we say no to a job, we will never get another one! I have done it. I am sure most of the profession has done it. Regrettably, what this leads to is lawyers taking on significant workloads and then trying to do it all themselves unless they embrace the concept of delegation.

Lawyers are sometimes reluctant to delegate for fear of losing a client to the up-and-coming young lawyer. The reality is that you will lose clients to up-and-coming young lawyers who have proven their mettle with the client. It means that you have to go and find another client to replace that one. But that is the way that the legal profession works. As one of my former partners wryly observed when we were discussing business development: "*All we are doing is stealing clients from one another.*"

I have mentioned these reasons not to denigrate those who express them as a reason not to delegate, but to highlight legitimate reasons why this occurs and why it holds back lawyers and law firms from growing appropriately.

When I got to a position in my law firms where I could influence who was going to be employed to work with me, I adopted the attitude of '*always employing someone smarter than me*'.

Of course, you never really know if someone is smarter than you. But once you have been around for a while, you can make an educated guess during the interview process about their level of intellect.

Why do I hold this view? Because if you have employed someone that is smarter than you, then you can delegate with confidence. You can delegate knowing that the work will come back to you at an acceptable standard. And generally, it will come back to you at a more than acceptable standard.

There is nothing better as a senior lawyer than when you are under pressure with work, being able to delegate the next job to someone smarter than you and not have to worry about that job getting done.

And as a senior lawyer, you can take pride in the advance of that junior lawyer through your firm, perhaps at another firm and through the legal profession.

And if there is ever an argument in favour of proper delegation it is that the pyramid structure of any substantial law firm works on the basis that senior lawyers get in the work and delegate it to less experienced lawyers to get it done, then charge for it. If your firm is set up that way, a failure to delegate properly will inevitably impact the growth and ultimately profitability of the firm.

Delegation is essential to '*working smarter not harder*'.

If you are a sole practitioner, or work in a firm with no employed solicitors, then how do you delegate when there is no one to delegate to? The answer to this is to analyse the various tasks that you perform during a day. Inevitably, a proportion of those tasks are administrative in nature, are bookkeeping tasks or are low level legal tasks. As much as possible, these should be delegated to employees to perform. It is a false economy to do all of this yourself when you can employ someone at a much cheaper hourly rate to do the work. This will free you up to do more legal work and from the profit that you make from the legal work, you can pay for the employee.

Too often I have seen sole practitioners who have enough work for one and half solicitors but will not employ a solicitor as they think they will not have enough work for both of them. Instead, they try and do all the work themselves leading to burnout, clients who complain about the lack of service and lack of contentment with legal practice. Far better to employ someone, delegate properly and have some spare time to devote to business development or even the spouse and the kids!

If this book was being written in 2020, I could have finished the chapter now. I cannot because artificial intelligence is at its most profound in its impact on delegation.

At its most elemental, artificial intelligence is the ability to use software and computing power to extract information from existing sources and apply that information to an issue. In 2020, I would have written that sentence as follows: '*At its most elemental, lawyers are used to extract information from existing sources and apply that information to an issue.'*

Looked at in that way, you can see what artificial intelligence can do for the legal profession and its impact upon delegation. Instead of delegating to junior lawyers, lawyers who harness the power of artificial intelligence and manage the risk that comes with it will be able to delegate those tasks to artificial intelligence through computer software packages.

Artificial intelligence will have an impact across the entire profession from sole practitioners to mega firms. But it poses its greatest risk to practitioners who use free artificial intelligence systems without the constraints and safety that comes from enterprise systems. The old adage of '*you get what you pay for*' is so true in this area.

But like everything in the legal profession artificial intelligence and its benefits will eventually trickle down and become affordable for sole practitioners and small firms.

In the context of this book, artificial intelligence will have the ability to remove drudgery from what we do every day and enable society to place value on attributes of the legal profession such as experience, nous and judgement. But, it also has the ability to remove the need to delegate to younger lawyers and train them in the art of the law. And in the long run, I fear that society will end up with not enough lawyers with experience, nous and judgement.

I hope that I am wrong in that assessment.

14

The art of earning a living

Getting the work and doing the work are essential but do not earn you a living. Getting paid for doing the work does.

Early in my career, one of my mentors said: "*If you're not going to get paid, you might as well be at the beach.*" How true.

Not getting paid is a double whammy. Firstly, you do not get the cash for your effort. Secondly, you have been denied the opportunity of doing work for someone else who will pay you.

The principle is the same whether you are a sole practitioner or a member of the largest law firm in the world. Not getting paid is a oneway street to insolvency. Of course, as a sole practitioner you have nowhere to hide if a client does not pay you. It has an instant impact on cash flow and profitability.

The larger the law firm, the greater the ability for a lawyer to hide behind the skirts of other members of the firm who are getting paid and generating the cash to keep the firm afloat. But even then, there is a day of reckoning, when the firm will no longer carry a lawyer who may do the work, meet budget but not get paid for the work that has been done.

Few firms have the courage to set budgets and remunerate partners and employees on the basis of cash in the door rather than bills out the door.

In the context of this book, contentment comes from getting paid for your work. It enables you to enjoy the fruits of your labour in other areas of your life, support your family and even invest some of it in superannuation or other investments.

So how do you make sure you get paid? There are some basic principles to follow. It does not guarantee payment and all of us have suffered bad debts in legal practice. But you should try!

We should all do pro bono work. It is the hallmark of the profession to do pro bono work for those less fortunate than us. However, you must make that decision before you do pro bono work so that you know who is going to be the recipient and how much you are prepared to do. Having a bad debt is not pro bono work.

So, the first principle is do your due diligence. Ask yourself the question at the start of the matter: '*How am I going to get paid*?'

If you are working for one of the major banks the answer to that question should be instantaneous. They have a history of paying your bills and you can be confident that they will continue to do so as long as you have done the work properly and in accordance with your fee estimate.

But if you are running a criminal practice, you should adopt the view of one of my colleagues in my firm who had a criminal practice: "*When the tears are in their eyes ask them for money upfront.*"

That was a very brutal way of saying that the only opportunity you may have to secure your fees is when the charge is looming and the courts are waiting. It is hard to recover money from a client occupying a gaol cell.

They are probably the extremes of due diligence. In between, you will have instances where you can only obtain payment when a settlement occurs, be it a family law settlement, a property or business sale settlement or a deceased estate settlement.

But the ones where lawyers have the most difficulty are where there is no pot of gold at the end of the rainbow and the client cannot fund the commercial or litigation matter as it goes along. Substantial costs may need to be incurred with the risk that if the matter does not go according to plan, you will be trying to get a client to pay a large bill and few resources from which to pay it.

Lawyers should always bear in mind what I call the '*parabola of discontent*' when deciding when to send an account to the client. I have chosen a litigation scenario to illustrate it but youcan see how it works in other types of matters as well.

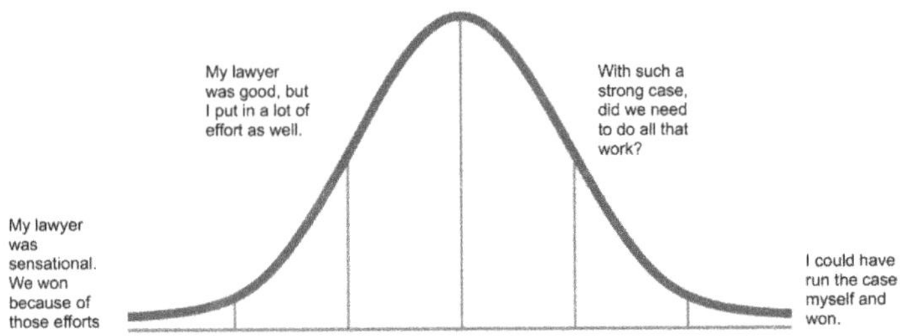

In a scenario where you have not been able to send interim accounts, it is imperative that you send an account at the start the parabola. If not, you risk the '*parabola of discontent*' encouraging your client to refuse to pay your account.

Lawyers are trained to help people and when a client has a legal issue, our focus is on how to resolve the legal issue. Far too often, I have seen lawyers jump straight into resolving the legal issue without thinking about how they are going to get paid if they do resolve the issue or worse still, if they do not resolve the issue.

Clients do not know the effort that has to go into resolving their legal issue. Not only the client who is engaging a lawyer for the first time, but sophisticated clients as well. The conduct rules require lawyers to provide realistic fee estimates of what it will cost to do a transaction or litigate the matter. This is meant to force lawyers to take a breath and think about what it will really cost and tell the client before incurring substantial fees. The continuing obligation to update fee estimates is also meant to help.

Lawyers are getting better at this, but in any substantial matter the variables in running the matter make it increasingly difficult to be accurate with fee estimates. The conduct of your client, the opposing client, the opposing lawyers and even the judiciary and the bureaucracy can easily blow out a well thought out fee estimate.

But a fee estimate still does not answer the fundamental question of how you are going to get paid for the work. It is one thing to give a fee estimate of $100,000 for a matter and have the client agree to that and quite another to get that amount of cash through the door.

Far too often, lawyers avoid this hard question by doing the work and sending an account at the end of the first month and see if that gets paid and continuing to work on the matter. My experience is that before you know it, you have done three months' worth of work on the matter, and you either have outstanding accounts or work in progress of a substantial amount. You cannot eat outstanding accounts or work in progress. You need payment.

So how do you avoid this problem?

Firstly, have the cost discussion with the client once you have a reasonable idea of what is the scope of the work. Sure, you might have to punt a couple of hours of your time if the client decides not to go ahead once it receives your estimate of what it will cost. Far better to lose a couple of hours of your time than hundreds of hours of your time in doing work which will not get paid.

In my experience, clients welcome an upfront discussion about fees. But as lawyers, we have no training in that area. At best, we learn by osmosis from an experienced colleague. More often than not, we hone our skills from having been burnt by clients and learning from our mistakes.

Lawyers are afraid of losing work if they tell the client how much it will cost. That is a risk, but one worth taking. Far better to be at the beach soaking up the vitamin D than working for a client that will not pay you.

When I practised in succession law, nearly every client always prefaced the telephone call or email about their estate planning saying that their will was simple and could I tell them what it would cost. I lost count of the number of times that I would say that I would need to know about their financial affairs to work out how complex the estate plan would be and therefore how much it would cost. I used to say that they would not ask a bricklayer to quote to build the front fence on the house without telling the bricklayer how long the fence was going to be and what type of bricks were going to be used. Despite what I thought was common sense, I was still getting pushback from the clients.

Accordingly, I abandoned that approach and told

clients that they could come in to see me, give me full instructions and once I had those, I would tell them what it would cost. I said that they could either agree the cost and I would do the estate plan, or they could disagree and I would not charge them a cent. How could they lose?

I only had to write off my time on two occasions with clients who you could describe as being *'careful with their money'*.

The lesson was that I was able to get every single enquiry into the office and have the opportunity to sell my ability to prepare an appropriate estate plan. More often than not, that ability and the savings to the client (or more particularly the beneficiaries of the client) more than justified my fee.

And getting proper instructions on the financial circumstances of the client was due diligence on their ability to pay me!

Secondly, do not be afraid to refuse to take on the work if you cannot see how you will be paid, or the risk of not getting paid is so great that you are effectively becoming the banker of the client. The responsibility for paying your fees rests with the client. Sometimes, you have to say to the client that you would love to help them, but you cannot see how they can afford to pay you, and you decline to act for the client. The alternative is to act for the client pro bono.

In short, you have to put the issue of your payment squarely in the lap of the client. If the client wants to have the legal problem resolved and wants you as their lawyer, leave it up to the client to work out a method of securing your payment. If that method is acceptable to you - great. If not, spend your time working for someone that can pay you.

As lawyers, we should put ourselves in the position of our clients. No client wants to, nor should be in the position of writing a blank cheque or electronic funds transfer for you to fill in as the matter goes along. When we retain other professionals such as dentists, doctors, architects and so on, we want to know what it will cost. When we get our house built, or we engage a tradesman, we ask for a quote. In all those cases, once we know that, we make the decision whether we go ahead or not. If you put your client in that position, sometimes you will lose the work. But if you get the work and get paid for the work it will make you a more contented lawyer. Let alone your spouse and your partners or employers at the law firm!

15

The art of client relationships

Clients. You can't live with them, and you can't live without them.

But clients are the lifeblood of the legal profession and having a proper and professional relationship with them is essential to a contented and rewarding career as a lawyer.

Clients come to us for help in resolving legal issues. Lawyers with legal issues are rarely clients of other lawyers. Most of us sort those out ourselves but we should always remember the adage of '*The lawyer who acts for himself or herself has a fool for a client*'. Most of us can see the legal issues early and act in a way which avoids the problem occurring in the first place.

So, lawyers rarely walk in the shoes of the client and see the issue from the client's perspective. Clients do not like spending money on lawyers. We are a necessary but reluctant spend to enable clients to access the law to resolve the legal issue.

Clients are under a degree of stress when instructing us. For some clients, the stress is substantial such as being incarcerated awaiting a criminal charge, marriage breakdown or sibling warfare upon the death of a parent. Commercial clients exhibit a degree of stress as well. Months of negotiation to strike a multimillion dollar merger and acquisition deal which can lead to a substantial financial benefit to your client inevitably means that your client is stressed to ensure that this happens. And generally, as soon as possible!

Lawyers need to appreciate that stress and empathise with the client. Again, no training is received on this during Law School and very little on a formal basis during your career. You are left to your own devices to pick it up by osmosis from other colleagues and educating yourself.

I count myself fortunate that some of my early mentors were simply good at empathising with clients and extracting the necessary instructions and giving clients the confidence that they were in good hands. As a junior lawyer, I watched in awe as they built rapport and respect from the client. As I said, '*The law is 50% know and 50% show*'. 50% show is what you need when giving the clients the confidence to entrust the legal issue to you.

On the other hand, I have witnessed lawyers who have exhibited narcissistic, patronising and downright rude attitudes towards their clients. If you want to know how that feels, remember when someone did that to you, such as an uncaring medical specialist or a snooty waiter who cannot understand why you want to put parmesan cheese on your spaghetti marinara.

So how do you empathise with the client? Remember that it is always the client's problem - not yours. Remain calm and focused on the client. Keep eye contact with the client. Do not raise your voice. Even if you must give some very firm advice and tell them they have a hopeless case.

Sometimes this is hard when clients, under considerable stress, need to vent. All of us have had clients who have directed their venom at us, not because they want to, but because we are in front of them and they are talking about something that is causing considerable stress to them.

Clients do not know what you need to know to help them. This means that when you ask a simple question such as: '*How can I help you?*' you are often met with an outpouring of words, sometimes with little coherence. When I practised in estate litigation, I used to call this the '*bowl of vomit*', which clients would fill up with what they considered to be the facts and then they gently pushed the bowl across the interview table for me to deal with.

The best strategy in those circumstances is to listen to that diatribe and then use that as a platform to obtain the detailed instructions that you need.

Building a rapport with clients is necessary, no matter whether you are defending them on a traffic charge or about to settle a multimillion dollar deal. Many of the things that I have talked about in this book such as communication, affability and knowledge are critical to build this rapport.

But rapport is a twoway street. As is respect for you from your client. If you are in a position where you can refuse to take instructions from a client, do not hesitate to draw the line in the sand if the client is not showing you respect or if there is no rapport. Do not be afraid to say to a client that you do not wish to act for them or that you no longer wish to act for them. It will save a lot of tears in the long run.

I have rarely had to do this. On one occasion, a new client came in to give me instructions and not long into the interview, he told me that he had dismissed his previous lawyer and then launched into a long speech about her alleged poor performance. I knew this lawyer very well and the allegations made were completely at odds with my experience in dealing with her over many matters. It was not long after this attack on the lawyer that the client filled the bowl of vomit. On this occasion, I declined to accept that bowl across the desk, and politely said that having heard what he had said, I did not think it was appropriate for me to act. I stood up, shook his hand and that was the end of that.

Building satisfactory professional relationships with your clients is not difficult. Most of it comes down to respect and empathy for the client. You may think everything is under control in the matter, but your client may not. Therefore, taking phone calls, promptly returning phone calls, promptly answering emails are the cornerstones of a professional relationship. Put yourself in the position of the client, and you can see that a few minutes of your time just to acknowledge that the client's issue is front of mind is a few minutes well spent.

As a rule, clients do not want to be your friend. Frankly, you should be careful if you want to be the friend of a client and still be their lawyer. By friend, I do not mean that you cannot accept an invitation from your client to go to the football and enjoy the largesse of the corporate box. It is more where the client invites you and your spouse to the client's home for dinner and drinks on a regular basis.

It is necessary to keep that professional distance so that you can give frank and fearless advice. You should never put yourself in the position where if you give frank and fearless advice, you risk losing a friend.

For that reason, refer family and friends to colleagues either within your firm or outside of your firm. You can keep an eye on the matter as a friend but leave it up to someone else to give the advice and do the work.

Do not think clients who are friends or family will not sue if you stuff it up. I know of one case where a lawyer at the end of a tennis match at his local tennis club gave some incorrect advice to one of the other club members. He got sued for professional negligence.

Sometimes, the client wants you as a friend or even as a friend with benefits. You may have the same feelings. If you do, you cannot be the lawyer for that client any longer and you need to refer the client somewhere else. You can then be a friend or a friend with benefits as you see fit.

If you do not have those feelings as a friend, politely decline invitations and if the client persists, you will need to say that you are happy to remain as the lawyer but cannot accept invitations as it puts you in a difficult professional position. If the client persists, then you need to terminate the retainer.

If the client wants you as a friend with benefits but you do not want a sexual relationship with the client, you can try the '*friend advice*' above. My preference is to simply say that even the implication of a sexual relationship compromises the professional relationship, and your client must see another lawyer. Sexual relationships do not mix well with professional relationships.

Although this is a chapter on client relationships, it goes without saying that non-consensual sexual approaches between practitioners is not on.

If you want the client as a friend or as a friend with benefits, the same rules apply. Refer them elsewhere for legal advice. In the case of a friend with benefits, make sure you do this before you enjoy the benefits. Given the professional risks, it would be wise to have at least an email from you referring your client elsewhere before you have sex. It goes without saying that you should not be typing this email as the bedroom door is closing.

Refer the client to someone outside of your legal firm. You do not want to be in the middle of a dispute between one of your business partners and your sexual partner.

Lawyers give advice. That means that you are not paid to agree with everything that the client has done or wants to do. You are paid to give advice to filter the law and apply it to the relevant facts of your client's case.

Inevitably, that means that occasionally you must give advice that the client does not wish to hear.

Not giving that advice often means that you are allowing your client to go along a path to nowhere and potentially at great expense to your client and possibly to you if your client refuses to pay your bill because you should have given frank and fearless advice earlier.

That is where keeping your professional distance from your client comes into play. Sometimes, you must deliver this advice face-to-face or on the telephone and that is never easy. Even after decades of legal practice, I still found this to be one of the most stressful parts of practice.

But on most occasions, you can deliver the advice in a letter or an email or by sending along a copy of a barrister's advice. At least then, the client has time to gather their thoughts before having a discussion with you. And do not be afraid to have that discussion. In fact, your last sentence of the email or the correspondence should invite the client to contact you to discuss the advice. Otherwise, you have just left the client hanging.

That is not good for current or future relationships.

It is always easier to deliver this type of advice to longstanding clients who through past dealings with you, generally respect your acumen and advice.

And it is a good practice management tool that if you must deliver this advice face-to-face or on the telephone, that you promptly confirm it in writing.

But just how do you deal with the difficult or demanding (or both) client? We have all had them. At some point in dealing with that client's matter, you will ask yourself: '*Why did I not see it coming?*'.

In my view, a difficult client is one that refuses to take your advice or wants you to tailor your advice to suit the outcome that they want. They telephone or email you incessantly and are sometimes abusive towards you or your colleagues.

A demanding client believes that they are your only client and that as soon as they need something done, you must do it immediately. They often set unrealistic deadlines. My experience is that if you meet the demands of this type of client, the matter goes silent and then the client wants the next part of the job done immediately even though they could have given you those instructions days before!

Assuming that you are in a position to decide whether or not to act for a client, the obvious answer is to do your due diligence before taking on the client. Of course, if the client is a major client of the firm, you may have no choice but to act. Nevertheless, if you are in a position to raise the unacceptable conduct of the client with partners or senior management, you should do so as if other people are having the same problems, the firm may decide to part ways with the client.

Even if you can pick and choose clients and their matters, it is no easy task to pick them in advance and refuse to accept the work. However, there are a few warning bells.

If the client has already fired their previous lawyer or the lawyer has fired the client, be cautious. If it is a lawyer that you know has a good reputation and is unlikely to have acted in the way that the client is saying, it is probably best not to act. At the very least, ask for money in trust to assess whether the client is really serious about the matter.

If you are the third lawyer that the client has hired, you should decline to act or at the very least do your due diligence by speaking to the other lawyers as to why they were fired. You are not obliged to act for a client: particularly one that will make your life a misery.

If you decline to act, do not refer the client to another lawyer. Save them the angst. Refer them to the Law Society or just stay silent.

Another warning bell is if the client wants to vigorously debate your initial advice. Nothing wrong with the client asking for clarification or explanation or putting you to the test of justifying your advice. But be wary of the client who does not want to hear what you have to say and prefers to follow the advice of other people who are advising in the background.

Make sure that your retainer agreements are set up

so that you can terminate in circumstances where advice is not being respected or followed, or if accounts are not paid on time.

One way of doing due diligence on the client is to find out how they were referred to you. The quality of the referrer can give you a good gauge on the potential quality of the client. If the client says that they found you by a website search or from advertising, ask them why they thought that you were the chosen one. The answer might lead you to ask a few more questions and get a better understanding of the psyche of the client.

If the client says that they want to litigate a particular matter on the basis of principle, be wary of taking on the client. By definition, the matter cannot be sorted by way of money changing hands and it can only be sorted by the principle being determined by the judiciary or an administrative body. Experience tells us that the principle diminishes in inverse proportion to the cumulative size of the legal bills. A disgruntled client is often the outcome.

But the truth is that difficult and demanding clients are part and parcel of legal practice. Terminating a client's retainer is both difficult and, in some firms, next to impossible. It is not the preferred option.

Despite what I have said above in relation to due diligence, the reality is that we have to deal with difficult and demanding clients. The worst thing you can do is put them in the too hard basket and not take their phone calls, answer their emails or correspondence and be dilatory in the conduct of the matter. You are asking for a hiding. In the worst case, you might find yourself as the subject of a complaint to the Legal Profession Conduct Commissioner.

The best way to deal with those sorts of clients is to take their phone calls, answer their emails promptly and so on. Deal with the matter properly and promptly. If the client keeps making incessant phone calls or sending numerous emails, tell them what you are charging every time they do so. It usually slows the client down.

The demanding client usually does not understand that you could not return their phone call that day because you are in an all day meeting for another client. A useful technique when that demanding client complains is to say that at some stage in that client's matter, you will have to devote a significant block of time to resolve their problem. You should say that you are sure that the client would appreciate your undivided attention on their matter and not conduct the rest of your legal practice when they are paying for your time.

In short, you have to suck it up whilst dealing with the matter. But having learnt your lesson, if you can, do not do any more work for that client. In large firms, you might even have to decline to act for that client and get someone else in the firm to do so - after giving fair warning to your colleague!

And then there is the client who sees nothing wrong with asking you to do something illegal or unethical. Just refuse. If the client will not take no for an answer, terminate the retainer. If you are in a firm where you are under pressure from above to do something which you consider is illegal or unethical, refuse to do so. Get some independent advice from someone senior or from the Law Society. Follow that advice. '*You only have one practising certificate but many jobs*' Keep that in mind.

16

The art of interacting with your colleagues

We spend an awful lot of our life interacting with other lawyers. They populate our workplace, the Bar, the Judiciary and Magistracy, administrative bodies, government and acting for the other side.

More than most professions, you are forced to interact with colleagues. Unlike many relationships in society, you cannot just think that someone is a tosser and remove them from your life. The cantankerous Magistrate hearing traffic prosecutions may be making your life hell as a lawyer representing your clients with traffic offences, but you can't just simply walk away when that is your livelihood.

Similarly, if you are in a firm which has a toxic culture, it is not easy to just walk away. But sometimes you must. Particularly if the toxic culture incorporates sexual harassment, bullying, discrimination and so on.

Having a fraught relationship with other members of the profession is incredibly stressful and underappreciated as a cause of unhappiness in lawyers.

So, what can you do about it?

Treat your colleagues with respect and courtesy - even if it is not returned. Do not stoop down to their level. Regrettably, there are lawyers who write aggressive letters and emails in the misguided belief that the lawyer on the other side will start quivering in their boots and give the aggressive lawyer's client everything they want.

There is nothing more delicious in legal practice than responding to this approach with respect and courtesy. It totally frustrates the aggressive lawyer.

Similarly, calmly respond to an aggressive telephone call from a colleague. But if the haranguing continues, you might have to say that you will not tolerate that type of language and that you are going to hang up. And then hang up. You have set the boundary, and the lawyer is unlikely to do it again.

Accept that there are some lawyers who have a personality which makes it very difficult to have a professional relationship with them. But you are getting paid by your client to deal with that person and you must do so in a professional way. Occasionally, I have had to deal with a lawyer with that type of personality. I found it very useful, after the telephone call, meeting or email to spend a few minutes with a colleague having a bit of a bitch session. Very cathartic and it helps to have someone else reinforce your view!

Other lawyers do not have to be your friend. If they are your friend, then in front of a client treat them as a professional colleague. A client expects that you will represent his or her interests without fear or favour. You are undermining your own reputation if at the start of the meeting, you are chatting with the other lawyer about how wonderful it was catching up with the other lawyer for dinner at a restaurant last Friday night. Of course, you should be polite to your colleague, shake hands (never give them a hug!) and you can engage in small talk.

If, by chance, the opposing lawyer is your friend, you should consider whether you should both refer the respective clients elsewhere within or outside your firm. Sometimes, the matter is such that you and the other lawyer can inform your respective clients and get their informed consent to continue to act. Disclosure is the key.

If you are married to or in a de facto relationship with the other lawyer you should never act, and you must refer the respective clients elsewhere. If you are having sex with the other lawyer or even exchanging flirty text messages, the same rule applies. Even if you stopped having sex with the other lawyer or exchanging the text messages - it won't cut the mustard if things go pear shaped.

Conversely, other lawyers are not your enemy. Do not allow your client to treat them like that or talk about them in a rude or condescending manner. Representing your client does not mean that you must let your client get away with treating a colleague in such a manner. It diminishes your reputation if you do.

When I was a young lawyer, I had a substantial family law practice. I was at the Family Court waiting to go into court with my client and present in the waiting room were the estranged spouse and his lawyer. Suddenly, and without any provocation the estranged spouse launched into a tirade of abuse directed towards me. The opposing lawyer did nothing and kept reading the brief. Luckily, the matter was called on and the tension dissipated. I was too young to take the other lawyer to task, but I gave up practising family law from that moment on.

The collective noun for lawyers is a '*gossip of lawyers*'. It is well known that managing lawyers is like herding cats. It therefore goes without saying that the dynamics of a law firm need to be carefully navigated.

Young lawyers, and indeed experienced lawyers joining law firms should tread cautiously. You will hear lots of gossip, but until you work out the factions and the dynamics it is best to keep your mouth shut. I am not encouraging you to gossip, but inevitably things will happen within the firm on which you will have an opinion. Sometimes you can share that opinion quite freely, but other times you can only share it with people that you trust. Trust takes time to build with other lawyers, but once established, having a colleague that you can trust with your opinions and confidential information is comforting.

But it is a two-way street. Do not use your trusted colleague as a dumping ground for everything that you want to say and then closing your ears and mind when your colleague has something to say.

And if a colleague has said something to you in confidence, maintain that confidence. Nothing destroys trust and friendship more than a breach of confidence - especially with lawyers.

One of the hallmarks of the legal profession is its camaraderie. Camaraderie is much easier with a smaller profession. Nevertheless, as the profession has grown, camaraderie tends to mainly exist between lawyers who practice within a particular area.

You should embrace this. On the surface, camaraderie may mean nothing more than a chat when you bump into a colleague in the street or catching up for a coffee after court. But it builds rapport and respect from your colleagues.

One day, when you need help it is much easier to reach out when you have built that camaraderie. In my experience, lawyers are very willing to assist colleagues who may be doing it tough. It might be the breakdown of your personal relationship, law firm partnership difficulties, a difficult client, a difficult matter or an ethical issue …

Whatever it might be, do not be afraid to reach out and ask for help. No one will laugh. No one will think less of you. A problem shared is a problem halved.

Law Societies have programs to assist lawyers with

these issues. Sometimes it is easier to discuss it with someone you have never met, but my experience is that if you know the character of the lawyer from whom you are seeking advice it makes it much easier to open up. It takes more courage to open up about problem than to bury it and hope that it goes away.

I have been the recipient of some great mentorship in my early years, and I have become a mentor as the years rolled on. But on not one occasion has this mentorship been formalised into a monthly meeting or anything like that. I think that this has worked because lawyers are busy people and having a monthly meeting might be more difficult to arrange and maintain than you think. Also, if there is nothing to discuss, then both the mentor and the mentee start to wonder if it is all worth the trouble. However, if you are fortunate enough to have someone who is prepared to meet monthly and you are also prepared to do so and make it worthwhile-go for it.

Lawyers love to solve problems. Therefore, if someone has a problem and needs to be mentored, lawyers spring into action at a moment's notice and provide the mentorship. Best left that way I think.

Although law firms can be '*interesting*' place to navigate relationships with other lawyers, conversely professional isolation from your colleagues can be a risk to your mental health.

Significant numbers of the legal profession practice as sole practitioners. Some of them practice in areas where they do not come across lawyers very often or at all as most of the work is client facing. Continuing professional development is now accessible by online seminar. Working from home rather than from serviced offices or chambers is growing. It is easy to become professionally isolated.

If this is happening to you, then make the effort to interact with the rest of the profession. You need to get the vibe of what is going on in the profession and build rapport and camaraderie for the reasons I have set out above.

Simple ways to achieve this are getting involved with the Law Society and its many committees, attending CPD seminars and workshops in person, and attending social functions organised by the Law Society.

If you do, I think you will be richer for the experience.

17

The art of being healthy

Legal practice makes it hard to stay physically and mentally healthy. Long hours, staring at a screen for hours on end, sitting down for hours on end and the weight of responsibility for another person's affairs are just the start. Throw in aggression from clients, colleagues, opposing lawyers and the judiciary and you have a recipe for poor health.

You might be able to survive all of this when you are young and fit, but as you age, it becomes increasingly difficult to look after yourself.

Nothing in the previous two paragraphs comes as a surprise to anyone who has been a lawyer for at least a few years. We all know that we must do better and that the rewards for maintaining good health are substantial.

But of course, it is easier said than done. All of us only have 24 hours in a day and if you happen to be employed by a firm that wants eight chargeable hours a day (which means at least 12 hours in the office), it is incredibly difficult to maintain good health. But even a small amount of effort is worth it.

Hopefully, this book has helped with your mental health and coping with the stresses and strains of legal practice.

But it is just as important to physically look after yourself. If for no other reason than it greatly assists your mental health. If you are physically fit, you do not get as easily tired at work, and it improves your ability to get through the work at an acceptable pace.

There are many lawyers who are fortunate to not only have the intellect which enables them to be a lawyer but have sporting ability to match. Most of us are not in that category. That does not mean that you do nothing.

An acquaintance of mine is a personal trainer. He said that keeping fit is not a matter of motivation but a matter of discipline. You simply must have the discipline to turn up and do the work. Whether it is a session at the gym at 6 AM or a long walk after dinner. If you have that discipline, you will get fit or stay fit.

There are a myriad of physical activities that you can do and this book is not the place to go through them!

I will limit myself to a couple of suggestions.

Do not underestimate the benefit of incidental exercise. Walk around the office as much as you can. Walk to meetings within a kilometre of the office. Walk to court if you can. Walk up the stairs rather than take the lift.

Have a lunch break and do not eat your lunch at your desk looking at the screen and typing emails in between a bite of a ham and cheese sandwich. Your brain needs a rest, and most firms have a lunchroom where you can enjoy your lunch, have a chat to some colleagues, read the paper or scroll the phone. If there is no lunchroom, the nearest park bench will do.

And when you have finished your lunch, go for a walk around the block. The fresh air will do you the world of good.

After doing that, you might feel the benefit of the endorphins and have the discipline to do more structured and vigorous exercise.

But all that can be easily undone by a poor diet and overindulgence in alcoholic drink and drugs.

Not everyone is fortunate to be a good cook or have a spouse who is. It is not easy when you and your spouse are both working fulltime and you must get a meal on the table every night. Let alone if you have children to feed as well.

It may be brutal advice, but you need to have the discipline to source, cook and eat good food. Whether that be that you spend Sunday afternoon cooking a few meals and putting them in the refrigerator for the week ahead or eating a bit later so that you have time to prepare a decent meal after you get home from work. You will feel better for the effort.

I appreciate that this may be very difficult to achieve if you and your partner are working long hours, have a long commute and are also trying to fit in with numerous other commitments that we have in life. It gets down to this. You need to prioritise your health. In the end, it is all that matters. If you have to rearrange things in your life or remove things from your life, then do so. If you don't want to do so, that's fine but just recognise that body keeps score.

When I was in my early 40s, I took my family on a fantastic holiday with some close friends to Bali. On the day before we left Bali, I left the others swimming around the hotel pool whilst I went shopping for some clothes. After doing this for a couple of hours, I was hungry and went into a food hall at the shopping centre for lunch. I caught typhoid from eating contaminated food. Typhoid has an incubation period of about a week, so I got sick in Australia. After two weeks of feeling like death warmed up, a physician finally diagnosed that I had contracted typhoid. As he neatly put it; it's often fatal, but don't be concerned-you are over the worst of it. I clearly remember thinking during that two weeks that if I could just get better, I would give up all of my worldly possessions.

Don't wait to catch your version of typhoid before prioritising your health.

When it comes to drink and drugs, it truly is a matter of discipline to not indulge. If you don't have that discipline, then you need to ask yourself whether you have an addiction and need formal treatment for it.

I know that is brutal advice and no one wants to hear

that they are addicted to drink or drugs or both. But the body does not lie. You can lie to yourself as much as you want, but eventually the body will tell you the truth.

18

The art of knowing when to retire

Legal practice is an all-consuming occupation. It takes up an enormous amount of time and when you throw in all the other things such as building and operating your practice, having a family life and a social life, it leaves limited time to develop any other substantial interests.

Many lawyers do have other interests outside the law. But most lawyers fear that these interests will not sustain them in retirement. There are plenty of lawyers who have no interests outside of the law or any interests are intricately involved with the legal practice. It is not surprising then that many lawyers are apprehensive about retirement.

This apprehension is perfectly understandable, particularly for successful and contented lawyers. They have enjoyed the intellectual challenge of being a lawyer. They have enjoyed the respect of their colleagues, the community and their clients. They have often been the centre of attention, and they have been relevant. They have been earning a decent income, particularly if they are still a partner or own the practice.

With retirement, the prospect is that all of that disappears and sometimes it disappears literally overnight.

What will they fill the time with? Do they have enough interests outside the law? Do they have enough friends outside the law or even within the law? How will they cope not putting on a suit and going to work but having to live cheek by jowl with their spouse? Have they saved enough money to see them through until death?

Retirement is different for everyone. When I was in my early 60s, I started to talk to other lawyers and professionals about retirement and what it meant for them. I was trying to work out in my own head what my retirement would look like and when I would retire.

It was a very worthwhile exercise. I came to realise that there is no right or wrong type of retirement - despite many books and articles trying to preach the 'perfect' retirement. I spoke to colleagues who were in their late 70s who were still practising about four days a week and still enjoying it. As one said, there is no point in retirement unless you have something better to do.

I spoke to colleagues who had retired in their early 60s and went straight from being a partner to being retired and loved the freedom and the lack of responsibility.

I spoke to friends in the medical and dental

professions who were able to do sessional work, go home and forget about work until the next session came along.

So, what did I learn? A few things.

Make sure that you are financially secure in retirement. If you are reading this book and your children have left home and you finally have some money left over at the end of the year, get some advice on how to invest it when you no longer have the cash flow of work. There are many excellent books available written for an Australian context. Read them. Educate yourself. Pay for some good advice.

Do not fret about not having enough hobbies or interests to sustain you in retirement. Few of us have. Retirement gives you the time and the freedom to have hobbies and interests develop organically. You might try something and you don't like it. Big deal. Try something else. Isn't that what we did before work when we had the time but not the money to explore interests? Now you have both the time and hopefully the money. So don't hold back!

Do not fret about a lack of intellectual stimulation. You will be surprised at how your intellect can adapt from drafting a complex clause in a contract to writing a book - such as this one! Other retired colleagues have been drafted into sitting on tribunals or advisory boards.

Do not plan everything that you are going to do in retirement. You are no longer at work and have to plan everything. Allow the universe to put things in front of you which you might like to do. One retired colleague has become an artist. He had never touched a paintbrush on a canvas in his life as a lawyer.

You might have retired as a lawyer, but that does not mean that you cannot take up some other enterprise which earns you a dollar. One of the great freedoms of retirement it is that you can do this as you see fit. You are no longer on the conveyor belt of earning a living and if you want to stop working for a couple of months for a trip overseas - you can do it. I know a few colleagues who became mediators or did sessional work on a tribunal once they retired from legal practice.

If you enjoy legal practice and you want to practice a few days a week - go for it. Remember that you have to still be as good a lawyer as if you are practising fulltime. Do not allow yourself to drift into the position where one of your inevitably junior colleagues must have the difficult conversation with you that your legal work is no longer up to scratch.

When I have spoken to colleagues about life after retirement, a consistent theme is the lifting of the weight of responsibility for other people's affairs. It takes a while to get into the rhythm of retirement. I was surprised at the number of retired colleagues who said that it took a few months to get out of the habit of jumping out of bed thinking about work.

So, my message is not to fear retirement. Think about it. Prepare for it. Enjoy it.

Appendix - Colloquialisms

Bang for your buck - value

Battery hen - working within strict guidelines

Beer and skittles - having a good time

Big end of town - corporate sector

Bitch session - intellectual discussion with a colleague about another colleague

Biting off more than you can chew - taking on more than you can achieve

Bright Spark - an intelligent person

Cracked the shits - had a tantrum

Cheek by Jowl - in close proximity

Chuffed - pleased

Cut the mustard - failure to reach an acceptable standard

End in tears - end in serious and perhaps irreparable dispute

Friend with benefits - sexual partner

Fucked it up - made a big mistake

Fish's Arse - incredibly small anus

Geez - wow

Get the drift-get the idea

Get this caper - understand this business

Give a stuff - care

Goalposts shifted dramatically - behavioural changes

Gruen - television show analysing marketing and advertising

Hang up the tools - stop practice as a lawyer

Hit the ground running - well-prepared

In the tent - supportive of a common goal

Nailed - perfected

Not up to scratch - not meeting an acceptable standard

Off piste - not sticking to the topic

On-the-fly - as it happens

On the slate - credit account

Pear-shaped - disastrous or very poor result

Play everything with a straight bat - doing something with the highest ethical and moral standards

Personality of a wet lettuce leaf - dour or morbid personality

Punt - bet or wager

Ring fencing - putting up a boundary

Rub of the matter - the truth

Saved my bacon - stopped a disastrous event

Sharpest tool in the shed - the most intelligent person

Sorting out the wheat from the chaff - the ability to remove poor performers

Spreading the butter too thinly across the bread - taking on too much responsibility or activity

Square peg smashed into a round hole - incompatible

Stabbed through the eye with a compass needle - enduring the greatest imaginable pain

Stuffed it up - made a mistake

Tosser - a person with undesirable personality traits

Two-way street - reciprocal respect

Upset the apple cart - become a disaster

Waxed lyrical - spoke glowingly

Won't cut it - failure

Working like a dog - working very hard

You beauty - great

www.ingramcontent.com/pod-product-compliance
Lightning Source LLC
LaVergne TN
LVHW050915210926
848482LV00012B/447